The Book of the Is

The Book of the Is

A book on bridges

Don't ask'em what it was,
tell'em what it is.

Phish

Bryan W. Brickner

ISBN: 978-1482518528

Made in the United States.

Table of Contents

Author's note ~

This book began in September 2001 and was completed in December 2004; President Bush had just been reelected to a second term and the war on terror was three years old. It has not been updated (there's no President Obama yet); it was edited for errors, misnomers and wordiness in 2012 and published in 2013.

Prefatory note

Dianna Brickner

What Is?

This is my experience . . . this is my Is. When I traveled a lot, that was my Is. I would fly from one city with its overcast sky and land in another city where that sun was shining. As I traveled, I realized that the sun was always shining above the clouds – until it sets – but it's shining somewhere! And it is beautiful!

A good friend taught me, "life is to express a character," and in doing so, you become the mapper of your own subjectivity. The Is fits in here nicely, as it is also subjective, like the sun, and it has continuous ongoings, just like the sun.

I think of this book as one of peace making and reconciliation. The Is is simple and complicated. In a simple, straightforward way, it just Is. This book points to bridges to aid in your journey. Use them, or not, as you are the one who can build the bridges to reconcile your Is. On this idea, another friend said: "The remnants of older bridges will fade as human knowledge increases, and the beginnings of new bridges will occur. But the Is insists, why wait?"

Then, in a complicated, "crooked-forward" way, many things shape your Is. Your roles and beliefs, daily situation and circumstances, education and income levels, health and spiritualism, all combine to form your Is. The Is celebrates the present without acknowledging the past or future. It uses the tools available to it and readily discards tools that are obsolete, without thought to what future tools might bring.

Think about it: how is it you know yourself? What, or where, is the origin of your religion, God, or energy? Do you still believe everything that you were taught, or has it changed for your perspective and taken on a life of its own? People talk of wanting to believe that someone is coming to save them – from what? From themselves? Yes, for some this may be a large part of their Is. We use the idea of reconciliation to come to terms with the world – whether it is through the lenses of Judaism, Islam, Christianity, Buddhism, or any other system of overcoming. How does overcoming the everyday form your Is?

In the United States we have a Constitution that guides us to a philosophy of what should be as set forth by our founders, those revolutionaries. Do you know the

Constitution? It spells out the structure in which the powers of the people, by the people, and for the people, are to be represented. Are we as a people constitutionally represented in the House of Representatives? In other words, does your vote count?

Do you "physically" know your body? It tells you a lot about yourself. What does your body say to you? It has ways of telling you that you over did it at the gym yesterday. It also tells you its preferences – hunger, thirst, desire, rest, and exercise, to name only a few.

Remember, the bridges, the things that connect to our Is, are offered here to use or not. A reader of *The Book of the Is* said: "The book's bridges consist of existing knowledge and resources that can take us to a better place in terms of difficult political issues; the bridges may not be complete and able to bear full weight yet, but the foundations have been grounded in realities from today's world."

In reading this book take note of two things:

1. Change is inevitable. Around 500 BC, a pre-Socratic philosopher, Heraclitus, noted: *"All entities move and nothing remains still."* Likewise, the Is evolves, ebbs and flows into something and nothing at the same time.

2. Reconciliation is hard work, but doable. We become attached to our being, or what we think we are, because we think that is what Is. We forget things change. You have to make others let you overcome your past, and actively work on doing so, to see what really Is: this is being. Learning to live with yourself is the greatest task, and formidable accomplishment, that you will experience. Enjoy your journey. The bridges are there to help you across.

Just go wherever it is that you have to with whatever it is that you have.

December 2004
Chicago

Introduction

> As regards Nietzsche, for example, it is we who have to honor his signature by interpreting his message and his legacy politically. On this condition, the signature contract and the autobiography will take place. It is rather paradoxical to think of an autobiography whose signature is entrusted to the other, one who comes along so late and is so unknown. But it is not Nietzche's [sic] originality that has put us in this situation. Every text answers to this structure. It is the structure of textuality in general. A text is signed only much later by the other. And this testamentary structure doesn't befall a text as if by accident, but constructs it. This is how a text comes about.
>
> *The Ear of the Other*, Jacques Derrida

The known changes, as what was known during the time of the US Civil War and what is known today is different.

The Is equals the known and unknown. This does not equal the truth, as knowns often conflict with other knowns. For example, the story of the prophet Abraham is known in many parts of the world, but its interpretation by various groups – Jews, Christians, and Muslims – is taken from different perspectives – the Old Testament, the New Testament, and the Qur'an.

The Is does not strip away myth for the sake of science, as that isn't the point; myth is as known as any science and science continues to evolve – just like myth.

It will be said that this is a heavy book, or that it is deep and abstract. It's not to me and my intention is that it will not be to you. To me, this book is base in both senses of the word – the lowest or bottom part, as well as having or proceeding from low moral standards. The Is is individual and whole, particular and universal. Even if there were no Is, there remains nothingness – and even nothing is a part of the Is.

This is not a book about my sanity. That has been established, at least sufficiently for me and for those immediately around me. No, this is about us, that relationship we have with others. You see, there has been an endless amount of work done on the ego. It is known as the frail yet seemingly all-powerful nexus of material life. The ego, with its 20th century flair for idealism and totalitarianism, is passé. Perhaps it was before its time;

the *e-go* would have been the perfect addition to the 21ˢᵗ century's bent for everything e- and high-speed. But then, it has a habit of being premature.

That is not to say that the ego can be discarded to the coming cultural revolution, as we haven't seen anything yet. The ego will survive, if you will, but its commanding presence will not.

The US Army typically devotes a whole day to a change of command ceremony, when really all that is needed are three officers, a US flag, and about five seconds. In this solemn ceremony, the present unit commander passes the stars and stripes to his or her superior officer, who then passes it to the (new) present commanding officer. The conferring moment, the moment of duty, rights, and responsibility as well as power, remains unbroken: the past, the higher, and the new. Said another way, the present, the present, and the present. Some conferring moments, such as Vice President Johnson's swearing in on Air Force One, come quickly and are marked by blood and violence.

The ego is no longer, by default, centric. That is because our world is no longer centered. It is still our world, but the geography is changing. From at least Copernicus, this has been an ongoing phenomenon that has bypassed religion in importance.

At conception, some say, life begins. What they are trying to say is that life begins way before birth. Condoleezza Rice, who at the time was President Bush's National Security Advisor, referred to slavery as America's birth defect. She was speaking, prior to the invasion of Iraq, about the US walkout from the 2002 United Nations conference on racism – the one where Arab states tried to portray Zionism as racist. Regarding our birth defect, her analysis only went so far. Our nation was conceived through war, in war, and by war. Those who founded the colonies warred on the aborigine; the terms "American Indian" or "Native American" are bemusing, both intimating a relationship, a naming, that only later became known, and the process itself elides another known (i.e., who they thought they were). Further, to break with Britain, we warred on our sovereign, King George. To the British, George Washington and his band of revolutionaries were traitors; to the aborigine, they were . . . well, what do you call someone who comes into your homeland and wars on your people?

Birds amaze us because of their ability to fly, but we admire them because they rarely fall. Unless dead or wounded, they always catch themselves. We, and here I mean everyone on earth, are never at rest. A virtue and default of life on this planet is the fact that we are constantly moving through the universe at nearly 67,000 miles per hour. No matter your activity, you are always whizzing through an incomprehensible amount of space and time. Movement is constant.

Work implies change, as it is nothing without it. Work also means that something is finite, like the sun. The sun works every day, but one day it won't. The sun's power is not infinite, not as we know it; science reports that the sun has about five billion years left of energy. They can see other suns that die in the universe, and then they look at ours and draw conclusions. Five billion years is a long time.

I've always found it difficult to think of God in philosophical or real terms. One way is infinite time and space. That is all well and good, but also inadequate. Both time and space necessitate something else, as neither can stand alone, which is what we expect from God.

Nature is never solidified and it is always in flux and dynamic – and yet people worship it. Culture is also worshipped and also never solidified. On this point, there is no difference between Nature and Culture; they are both based on change. We think falsely when we imagine either as constant. The former, which carries the latter at 67,000 mph, or about 19 miles per second, is thought to be the slow one; but, as was just said, they move at the same speed.

This movement points to space, time and thinking. Thinking is a biologically juiced mix of chemicals powered by a mass of brain cells. This makes it dimensional, or wholly dimensional. So thinking passes as the flip side, and along the lines of, the inhalation's exhalation. In a gross way, thinking is puking, sort of, only there's more spewing and sucking.

Does it make any sense to say we will only protect Nature when we think it is in our best interest? We burn fires to warm the cold, build needed shelter, and eat what is edible. Our place in Nature has always been synoptic – a summary from the same point of view. Synoptically, you could say, like the first three chapters of the Gospels – Matthew, Mark and Luke – we tell familiar yet different stories.

In proceeding, it might be helpful to imagine a circle you can enter from any direction, and let that be your guide; it builds a sort of anything goes into the process and keeps it entertaining.

December 2004
Chicago

1

Omphalos

1. *Anat.* The navel.
2. A central part; focal point. [Gk.]

1

In the beginning, there was the Is. It doesn't matter how you imagine the Is, either through the prophets, the evolution of the known (science), or by another way, the Is remains. The Is, for definitional purposes only, is sense and chemicals, especially neurotransmitters, which are the chemical base of consciousness. The Is was and is mine and everyone else's, and it has always been that way.

The Book of the Is is an incomplete book. It is touted as being on bridges, but only in a loose and general way. The bridges are things that connect, like beginnings. These are both internal and external, as far as that distinction makes sense, because we will come to see that the internal and external are more or less similar. An example of an internal bridge is a neurotransmitter. An example of an external bridge could be an airplane ride or as simple as holding someone's hand.

This is an incomplete book because the Is cannot be completed in any traditional sense of the word; like a circle, rather, the Is is always already complete and all the while awaiting completion.

Let us start with the umbilical cord, that tether and lifeline to our initial reality. Born into this world from another one, tethered to an old reality, and in moments the initiation commences, but do we ever not know that? I mean we find ourselves every day, just like the day before, yet different altogether. Beginnings? No, there are no beginnings, no endings: things commence and then they don't.

2

To the ancient Greeks, Delphi was known as the center of the world. The story goes that Zeus, in order to find the center of the world, let loose two eagles. One flew from the east and one from the west. They met at Delphi.

At the time of the ancient Greeks, they invented a religious system at Delphi based on the prophetic musings of the Pythia. More precisely, this is where the god Apollo spoke to humans.

The Pythia was a woman and, according to ancient sources as reliable as Plutarch, a male priest at Delphi and later historian, the Pythia gained her oracle state after inhaling a gas from a fissure in the temple of Apollo, the god of prophecy. Modern science now reports that the old evidence is true. It doesn't take much imagination to connect the two: the most important site of the Greek religion was based (built) on "getting high."

What a lovely concept this "getting high," and yet it isn't always looked kindly upon. The problem is in the fact that getting high isn't transcendental. You do not transcend the moment (time) when high, so in that regard it is not transcending. Getting high is a body experience and therefore always in time. The last great Christian philosopher, Immanuel Kant, set the standard we generally use for transcendental: *knowledge that is beyond the limits of experience.*

Clearly, getting high is an experience. For those who have ever been high – defined as you will – it is certainly an experience, and there doesn't seem to be any doubt about that. An experience, understood basically, is a sense~chemical reaction in the body. This means both have to be present: sense and chemicals (neurotransmitters).

Getting high is also not always, though some would disagree, transcendental in another important sense of the word; getting high is not based on and does not privilege *a priori* knowledge. We say the word "American" and expect it to mean something; this is also true of transcendental. For example, monotheism is transcendental and points to *a priori* knowledge – think prior or pre-knowledge. This isn't intuition, as that is the putting together of knowledge and not pre-knowledge. As we will see below, *a priori* knowledge lacks wisdom in the sense of not knowing. No one knows what was known before the known. Monotheism provides an answer to this vacuum with the story of a day of Judgement. You will also notice the Abrahamic trilogy (Judaism, Christianity and Islam) share the common knowledge of sin and the garden of Eden, the omphalos of monotheism.

3

Delphi was a religious site even before Apollo slew the Python and made its power his own. Stories before stories – that just tells me this issue of consciousness has been an ongoing one. *What are humans?* We could begin with a concept of adaptation: not much of a definition, but good enough for now. As we will come to know, humans are not that well defined. If anything, our latest economic system, the market, is built on this undefined aspect we call human nature. The Is that humans create has, seemingly, become more complicated – faster if you will. With the death of God we face another crisis, this one, as all the others, one of value. How is it that one value outlasts another? How is it that any society becomes less or more of anything? And what *of* all this For *and* Against?

There is an Army television ad being played this time of year. With football weekends, the World Series, and the presidential campaign, it is a few months where the flag, patriotism, and the military really sing the same song. I was taken in by them in my youth, and still am occasionally.

The Army ad in question is instructive on where ideas come from. (And no, I'm not blaming the media – humans do as humans do: if there is a morality to this book, that is it.) The ad shows an Arab man walking down a dusty road with a rifle slung over his shoulder; the man also has scope-sites across his chest, making him a target. The television watcher has the rifle-toting Arab in his/her sites – the kill zone.

The ad is well designed for its target audience. Learning to kill is the first mission of the Army and any soldier; that is what war is about. Even though well designed and effective, the ad was revolting. I understand that liberty is often born out of violence. I was commissioned an officer in the US Army, so I was even trained in the use of violence. To be free, many have and will continue to take up arms. It is the enemy-creating power of the ad that I found revolting, the power to make killing okay; somehow the enemy justifies the practice. There must have been a footnote to God's Ten Commandments, those given to Moses. Perhaps it couldn't fit on the bottom of the two rock slabs; or maybe Moses left it on the mountain. But the footnote must have looked like this: Thou Shalt Not Kill – *Unless Thou Has A Really Good Reason.

That's how we killed God: we challenged "him" and talked ourselves into a new way. We killed God with our questions and keep him alive in our prayers. We aren't that aware of this yet, but it's different now, which I think we know, and there's no going back.

4

The adaptable human explains the basis for organized life, thus forming a central part of activity. One can imagine a human beginning; the brain awakens to new sounds, new experiences, and new codes. The codes are repeated the next day and the next, until the pattern is normalized into a gesture or sound. These chemical events become conscious to us.

Because all animals adapt, we have to say more about humans to differentiate us by degrees, if nothing else, from other animals. The differences are found in the way we process chemicals, as it is this mix that makes us unique. Our consciousness is sometimes called a "higher level," or something to that effect; what is meant is more complex. That seems to be the case. Physically, consciousness (thought) is formed in the synaptic exchanges between brain cells. With chemicals and electricity, the body makes consciousness. That's the physical part.

In one way, I think that is what happened to "Abram." That's what Abraham was called before he received God's covenant and was circumcised; that's when he became Abraham. So, Abram was conscious and had an experience. He became the first of what we call the prophets of monotheism. The prophets have taught *a priori* knowledge – God's knowledge. They have changed the world with their words – God's words. In order to do so, science says, some chemicals combined or were lacking – things like serotonin, norepinephrine, and anandamide (human names for God's creations) – naturally occurring, that is, chemicals produced by the body to be used in processing sense – consciousness – thinking – words.

Every prophet of the Abrahamic trilogy has taught the same lessons. They had similar conscious experiences that they found to be transcendental. In one sense, this means they were experiences that couldn't be explained – unknowable is a word they may have used. But that doesn't go far enough. What the prophets of monotheism have taught and what we have learned is that there will be a day of Judgement; that we will have that experience and that experience matters. This is repeated over and over and taught again and again: Abraham, Ishmael, Isaac, Moses, Jesus, and Muhammad, and all the others. I know there are questions of legitimacy concerning Jesus and Muhammad, as well as Ishmael and others, as prophets of monotheism; that does not invalidate the fact that they taught the same lessons concerning justice and the day of Judgement.

So it is chemicals that differentiate us from other animals and from the prophets – the prophets of monotheism that is. The Pythia at the Delphic Oracle is another story. Rather than God finding and hailing the prophet, the Pythia was recruited, trained and thought to channel the power of Apollo, the Greek god of prophecy; how different an arrangement that was.

The Pythia was always a woman from Delphi. She had few other requirements that concerned her standing in Greek culture. Her age didn't matter, for instance, and neither did her wealth. She had to prepare for the oracle sessions: this seems to have required fasting and no sex. The gas turns out to have been ethylene; it rose from a double fault line under the temple; a fissure underneath the tripod-seat of the Pythia allowed the chamber to fill with gas. When taken in small doses regulated by time, the Pythia would enter into a slight trance. Individuals from the simple to the great would come to ask her questions. Delphi became the center of the world not for the power of *a priori* knowledge, but because of experiential knowledge, which is called *a posteriori* knowledge (think of the prefix post-). It should be noted that before asking the question of the Pythia, the questioner had to perform a ritual bath and sacrifice an animal; if the entrails quivered when splashed with water, the questioner was turned away from the temple and did not meet with the Pythia. Like the Old Testament, the temple of Apollo paid homage to animal sacrifice.

The prophets of monotheism told us about God's knowledge and a day of Judgement; the prophets of Apollo, the Pythias, told us about world affairs. Ironically, perhaps, most of this was going on at the same time and within a thousand miles or so. Abraham to Muhammad runs from the early second millennium to 632 AD. There were temples in operation at Delphi from around 1100 BC until approximately 200 AD, at which time the ethylene gas disappeared.

It was said the Pythia: "neither conceals nor reveals the truth, but only hints at it." A king learned that lesson the hard way. King Croesus of Lydia asked the Pythia if he should invade his enemy, Persia. The Pythia responded that a great empire would fall; King Croesus invaded not knowing *his* was the falling empire.

The Pythia had no prior knowledge of the king's impending defeat because it wasn't impending at all – it was his call, and he made the choice. That was how the Pythia worked: she wasn't a prophet of *a priori* knowledge, of transcendental knowledge, but a prophet of experience. She answered your question and let you be on your way; her morality was your morality.

5

The Is for the prophets of monotheism and for the Pythia were obviously different, but it is the similarity that interest me now. The Is cannot be only or just monotheism. The Is cannot be only or just ethylene gas. What Abraham and the Pythia shared, for example, were sense and chemicals. I do not know what happened to Abraham when Yahweh spoke to him with two angels (Yahweh/God didn't come alone, we are told). I also don't know what happened to the Pythia when Apollo spoke through her and the gas. What I do know is that they both had experiences, physical brain experiences, sense~chemical moments, that were and still are, real.

6

I should explain what I mean by the phrase "sense~chemical." The Book of the Is is written to be a readable American book. That said, I will keep answering various questions until the idea is become ideal. All ideals have a counter, an opposite if you will. In this case, to get close to a world that isn't monotheistic, we have to create another idea, another value. Luckily, that is what humans do best – adapt. Take the pairing of sense~chemical: it is a way to describe the workings of consciousness. Put simply, science has progressed to the point of a theory of consciousness. This isn't *a priori* knowledge: this is *a posteriori* knowledge. The difference is between some guarantor of knowledge – like God, Reason, or pure thought – and no guarantor of knowledge, not in the monotheistic day of Judgement sense. Value is human; the only guarantor of knowledge is experience, which changes, constantly.

If you think things can't work without a guarantor, think about the American system of money. At one time, and not that long ago, the US kept enough gold in Ft. Knox to back up our paper money – a sort of one to one ratio. Nixon changed all of this by executive order in the early 70s. Just like that, no guarantor of money and yet the system functions quite well. Of course, some day it won't, as nothing human has permanence. Even biology, or the naming of body processes, lacks permanence.

For all the commotion it has caused, consciousness actually functions rather simply. There was a lesson I taught to my high school students. In more than a decade of teaching, one witnesses that the brain is capable of vast amounts of learning. As this process continually impressed me, I wanted to know the mechanics – I wanted to know how it worked. One could think the process is driven by unknowable forces: I don't know what sparks the drive to be the individuals we are; I do know we learn, and I wanted to be able to describe – to teach – the biology of that process to my students. I thought if they knew what made the proverbial light come on – the "Ah, hah!" moment of learning – I thought if they knew how that worked they'd be better prepared. That's teaching to me, when something is communicated to someone, when something is learned; I wanted to know how that worked.

What I learned and passed along to the ninth graders was the following. After drawing two brain cells on the marker board, I would identify the three parts of every brain cell: axon, dendrite and soma. Axons carry information away from the soma; dendrites bring information to the soma. Cells pass electricity and chemicals called neurotransmitters and neuromodulators. Fancy words, but they are chemicals that help in thinking; they help in transmitting electrical signals and in modulating moods. These chemicals are released from the axon into the synaptic cleft; this is the space between two cells. In this gap, the electricity and neurotransmitters (sense and chemicals) pass between cells. The "Ah, hah!" experience is an example of when a new thought has occurred and the student learned. (Retention is another matter; here the point is how a thought is created.) An example outside of teaching and one we all have probably had, is an orgasm; the rush in the brain (and elsewhere!) is way more than a simple "Ah, hah!" – wouldn't you agree? And think how television makes your brain waves dull and lifeless – the couch-potatoing effect. Those are the effects I'm talking about.

This is only one part of consciousness – the base-building blocks. Science tells us there are over 100 billion brain cells; the one-synapse and chemical release between two cells is only a part of the process; it is the sequencing between thousands and millions of cells, played out biologically, which make our thoughts. One other interesting point: cells have a positive and/or negative (plus and/or minus) electrical charge. It is out of the combination of electrical currents (so many plusses and so many minuses) and chemicals that thought takes place; there is no thought (meaning no pure thought, you Kantians) without the body having a sense~chemical experience. Thought is *biologic*.

I would then talk about how electric our bodies are, how we are electric beings. Commonly, I would use the ER scene where they are trying to revive a patient who has "flat-lined." The patient is shocked in order to resuscitate – to restore consciousness, vigor or life. (Resurrect is to bring back to life, raise from the dead.) The human is shocked to bring the body back online; if there is no current, no electricity firing the synapses, then, in less than a minute or so, there is no life.

From there we would move to a discussion of the brain and body. Specifically, how does the body communicate? How does the foot know what the hand is doing? How is it I can write on the board? We discussed those kinds of questions. First, the students would consistently think the answer was blood. Of course, this is partly true. Often, I would do something out of the norm – such as one push-up – and then ask them how my body was able to do that?

The nerves they would say, and that moved the discussion to the brain. If the nerves (our senses) are sending and receiving information, how is the brain processing the signals? I would tell them, getting the electricity to send the signals is only part of the equation; the other part is chemical. This would actually lead to a discussion of why they should eat a good diet and why they shouldn't use drugs. It also was the occasion when they would discuss some of the drugs they were on or had taken – Ritalin, for example, or an opiate from a surgery. Students know a lot about drugs and have lots of questions.

The "Ah, hah!" moments, the moments when the "light comes on," the moments we recreate memories, these are the passing of electricity and chemicals between thousands and millions of brain cells; it is this sense~chemical combination that is consciousness. Diet becomes a big issue when thinking of thought in these terms. Think how a diet high in sugar, caffeine, nicotine or alcohol would affect and effect the sense~chemical combinations. (Neurotransmitters aren't created out of nothing; they have precursors.) Or think how a diet of fasting, one where key neurotransmitters may be absent or overabundant, and think how that might affect and effect the sense~chemical combinations. The point is that diet and sense, chemicals and electricity, that is the biology of consciousness as we know it today. *Consciousness is a sense~chemical experience; it's in the bridging across synaptic clefts that humanity was created, that is, first felt.*

7

This chapter is an attempt to provide a bookend, a countervalue, to monotheism. Monotheism is a form of "mono-thinking" (the idea that there is a One). Chapters two through four keep the bookend, countervalue theme going by discussing messiahs, the US Constitution, and the human body. As we go on, I've noticed that when thinking about the Is it does help to think of a circle – it's because a circle has no sides. Calling the Is amoral – without morals or sides – wouldn't be accurate though. Values are human made, and since they are made – the German word *gemacht* comes to mind – they are moral. It cannot be helped, as it is human and that is always already moral. We come into this world through care, some better than others, but still some level of care. That's just one example of what I mean by always already moral, as care is there from the beginning.

This also isn't an atheistic book – a book about a world without God – but people may think it so. God is dead means monotheism is dead. God is dead means there is no premised day of Judgement: there is no guarantor of value. The Is has to be approached this way – from a premise and not a promise – as a means to discussion. Monotheism needs a counter balance, one beyond good and evil, one with experiential value. Think of the Super Bowl or World Series: they both take two to tango, two to enter the fray, two to create value. Mono (the 1) doesn't need competition though – it doesn't need *more* gods. What is needed is a modern –1, which is *not* necessarily the equivalent of Satan or evil, but opposite and different: nonetheless, some will call it evil. It might be that monotheism needs a premise, a new premise, and we humans, as well, need to clarify some things. So, that is what we will do, as this ideal will be our omphalos, our belly button, the place we begin and began.

8

It does no good to say one thing and then to do another. Your word becomes a false promise if you do. Like the athlete who predicts victory and then fumbles it away, we like this about ourselves – our brashness and willingness to fail – as it too has served us well, even when we fumble it away.

A family is really a tale of how we were raised. When she was an early teen, my future maternal grandmother was sent "down the road" to another farm, where she lived and worked for several years. What began out of necessity became a custom, as putting the children to work wasn't only an option, but a true solution to how to feed them.

My family story hails from Germany. Both sides trace their beginnings to the immigrations that occurred after the 1848 revolutions in Europe. So, about 1852, they started arriving in northwestern Illinois and southwestern Wisconsin. This was farmland and they made a living. One tale I was told was that the one side came to America as Mennonites. I had to look this up, but I knew it was a Christian group. A Mennonite is defined as: *"a member of an evangelical protestant Christian sect opposed to taking oaths, holding public office, or performing military service."* By the 1900s, the Mennonites had become Presbyterians. I guess that might mean they could now take oaths, hold public office, and perform military service. I'm sure of one thing: my grandmother spoke fondly of "Tippy," her cousin who was killed while on a bombing run over Germany in 1945. Ironic, I suppose, but that is how things work. The kin of German Mennonites return to Germany as Presbyterians (and Lutherans, Methodists, and Catholics, I'm sure) and bomb their former kin and homeland. That's powerful to think that the "ideas" of the United States – patriotism if you will – could have such effect in only a few generations. Former non-military serving Germans returning to Germany to defend, fight, kill and die for America. Amazing, really, to see it work like that.

9

That is the Is, and we have to get at it like that and in this manner. In this chapter, monotheism completes the circle, so to speak, and that is the challenge the Is must take up. Recall the discussion of 1 and –1 and how they don't negate each other as much as hold each other in place – in check. We wouldn't think of calling –1 evil just because it stands in opposition to 1. Minus 1 is not the evil opposite of 1, the same way the Is is not the evil opposite of monotheism: different yes, evil no.

I suppose it is clear why some will call this an evil book; experience teaches that it is part of our humanness. But remember 1 and –1, and you may not think it so evil.

In *Human, All Too Human – A book for free spirits* (1878), Friedrich Nietzsche wrote in aphorism 99: *"force precedes morality"* and that *"indeed, for a time morality itself is force, to which others acquiesce to avoid unpleasure."* This is one of those key texts for me in understanding a way of thinking. In monotheistic texts, there are also many that propel thought, such as Romans 12:17-21, Genesis 1:29, and Surah 23:33-38. At this point in Nietzsche's text, he has drawn conclusions about morality. (He also premised a death of God theory . . . some say it even started with him, but it's been around – he just did it well.) *Force precedes morality* is saying whatever is being played out between humans always involves force. Force can be something from the outside, like the police, or something from the inside, like a conscience. You'll notice both require the sense~chemical combination to reach a level of consciousness we call aware. No one gains recognition of rules and order without bringing those ideas to life – to consciousness. Rules and order must be recognizable to us. Since force is an external and internal experience – always already – then how it is made conscious and recalled becomes the key. Driving in America is a good example of how this works, how rules and order come together. Over the course of driving, it seems that sooner or later, given the statistics, all drivers will have occasion to communicate with a police officer – a representative of force, so to speak. A common meeting is a traffic stop for speeding; the force element appears in the flashing lights and siren. Senses become aware and responsive in both the police vehicle and in the car being pulled over. In this example, force comes upon a driver and, in most cases, the driver pulls aside and the situation is resolved. Either a ticket is issued or an understanding is reached (such as, *"Slow down"*).

Conscience, the good and bad, works the same way and at the same time. As the brain receives information (flashing lights and siren), some people choose to run. They step on the gas and a chase ensues. We won't write the ending of the chase because it isn't the key moment. The key moment of force is the dual failing/opening: a bridge fails one way and opens another. There we see force at work, where it puts its cards on the table. In this moment it isn't God or morality that has failed, only a certain kind of force has failed – the force of social convention. (By the way, this is the same force that allows most of us to drive ten miles per hour over the speed limit – at least in your home state.)

Nietzsche goes on to say force: *"becomes custom, and still later free obedience, and finally almost instinct."* I think he's correct. In essence, we have to be forced to be moral; we have to be forced to care. This can come from within or without, internal or external force, but it comes down to a sense~chemical moment and a decision is made. I don't find or feel monotheism present in these moments, as some do, I know. What is clear is that the prophets of monotheism understood *force precedes morality*. Part of God's promise to Abram involved the act of circumcision. Force is convincing, and monotheism has convinced billions.

Nietzsche closed with this: force become instinct, *"is coupled to pleasure, like all habitual and natural things, and is now called* virtue.*"*

If we pull over for the police, we are being virtuous; we accept our actions and proceed accordingly. So this force, custom, free obedience, almost instinct, now called virtue route – well, it's so human. Does anyone doubt it is humans who make virtues? Humans make this stuff up. I'm supposing for the monotheists that it becomes a question of who made humans? Who made the sense~chemical bridge?

10

I want to write about Hud; he's a lesser-known prophet of monotheism, but a decisive man of God. According to the stories of the prophets, Hud was born five generations after Noah (*Nuh* in Arabic). He is spoken of in the Old Testament as "Heber" and is the great-grandson of Noah's son Shem (Genesis 46:17).

In Hud's life, the people had turned away from monotheism again and returned to worshipping stone idols. Apparently, as humans are prone to do, the promise made to Abraham wasn't enough, nor the words of Noah or the destruction of the world by God: once again the stone idol worshipping returned.

Hud preached the message of monotheism. In Surah 23, called "The Believers (*Moaminun*)," Hud is challenged by the local official and called a liar. Now, you can get away with a lot in the Old Testament, New Testament and Qur'an, but calling a prophet of monotheism a liar usually signifies a bad move. In the Surah – a Surah is a collection of verses in the Qur'an – we are told that the leader of the idolaters, in verse 38, says this about Hud: *"He is naught but a man who has forged a lie against Allah, and we are not going to believe him."*

In verses 39-40, Hud asks for God's help in standing up to their lies and is presented as saying: *"In a little while they will most certainly be repenting."*

Well, Hud got most of it right. The story tells us that the disbelievers in monotheism wouldn't listen to Hud and that God sent a drought. Still later, after the drought, the disbelievers still wouldn't believe. Finally, since they wouldn't stop believing in their stone idols and wouldn't believe in the promise of monotheism, they were all destroyed in a large storm. Hud and some other believers survived. This story is said to have taken place five generations – a couple hundred years or so – after the great flood of Noah's time.

Let's return to a point in verse 38. The local official is described as a worshipper of stone idols, and yet he says something of interest; he says that Hud is a man who has created a lie *against* Allah. The idol worshipper, the worshipper of stone, interestingly, isn't preaching against Allah or monotheism in theory: he is accusing Hud of a lie. He's not saying there is no Allah; the stone worshipper and his people weren't destroyed for not believing in the theory of monotheism, *per se*; they were destroyed for not believing in the resurrection and the day of Judgement that goes with it. In Surah 23, verses 35-37, the chief of the stone worshippers says this about Hud and his message:

> 35: What! Does he [Hud] threaten you that when you are dead and
>   become dust and bones that you shall then be brought forth?
> 36: Far, far is that which you are threatened with.
> 37: There is but our life in this world; we die and we live and we
>   shall not be raised again.

For denying the teaching of the resurrection, that is what got the stone worshippers killed by the great storm. They didn't deny Allah: the worshippers of stone denied the resurrection. *A priori? A posteriori?* Remember those? Hud was a prophet of prior knowledge; the resurrection is needed for the day of Judgement – no resurrection, no day of Judgement is possible, as the body is needed for heaven and hell (at least the hell part). The resurrection, the raising of the dead, wasn't compelling to the stone worshippers – not even a drought convinced them.

11

Being for something might be easier than being against something. They are equal in theory, but the negative energy of being against is often detrimental to humans. I'm thinking of Bush and Kerry here, as examples. I could first vote for the president in 1984 and voted for Ronald Reagan. Since then it has gone like this: George Bush, Bill Clinton, didn't vote, Al Gore, and John Kerry. Three out of five isn't bad, and being on the losing side isn't bad either. A turning point for me was the time spent in Saudi Arabia in 1991: Army time, battalion staff officer, post-conflict (peaceful), July to November. In 2004, the *for* Bush were stronger than the *against* Bush. It works both ways – the against win just as often – but this time the *for* side won. Good work.

Perhaps the challengers of Hud, the ones who called him a liar – actually, a creator of a lie against Allah – perhaps they repented in death. It gets hard to know. I don't take the central mark of monotheism to be a vengeful God saga. That's not the point: the stories are there and they can be instructive – that's why they've been passed along. By today's standards, our modern ways, God's wrath for a refusal to believe appears harsh. Others would say it is a harsh world.

But there's a conflict between knowing and the future. Anyone who gambles knows there is risk involved in betting. Well-experienced gamblers, even the professionals, often lose. See how *a priori* knowledge isn't welcomed. It's called cheating – like stacking the deck or loaded dice. In the old days, they'd shoot you; now they just ban you from casinos. You find the gambler's swagger in the prophets of monotheism. They believed and were betting their existence on God's promise. They have the swagger of insider information – not cheating mind you – but someone who believes they are going to persevere – someone who feels their way of thinking will win.

The stacked deck the prophets used was simply an ordering of value. They knew, through God's promise to Abraham, what the outcome would be. They didn't admonish God's time or manner, but they persevered. They abided by God's law, prayed, and carried on. Hud waited for God to get the stone worshippers, he didn't do it himself.

You can see the tension. The tension is between patience and action. I think Hud showed wisdom in being patient. The wise, according to one of the legendary answers of the Pythia, the wise do not know. Hud believed in God and asked God for the strength to be patient. He didn't pretend to know what God's plan was for the stone worshippers, and that made him wise.

12

Socrates is one of those monumental Greeks. He taught the *maieutic* method: this meant a bringing forth of truth through the method of question and answer. In Greek, the word means to act as a midwife. It works by helping an idea along to its, well, birth. He said once that Aspasia taught him the method. She was a teacher from Asia who was the beloved of Pericles, a great general and leader for the Greek city of Athens from 458 until his death in 429 BC. It all went well for a while, but Athens eventually lost the Greek wars. Socrates was sentenced to death by Athens in 399 BC for corrupting the young with his teachings. They gave him the option of banishment from the city or suicide by drinking poison – hemlock. He surprised them (or made their day!) by drinking the hemlock. Score one for sacrifice.

Socrates wasn't a writer, so what we know of his thoughts are passed to us from others. The Pythia at Delphi reportedly said something interesting about him. As I mentioned above, the Pythia was asked who was the wisest person? She responded that Socrates is the wisest because he knows he doesn't know.

There goes that Pythia again, never being very clear – the wise as those who don't know? That looks wrong, doesn't it? If that's true, then what are the dumb, right? – The one's who know?

See, it's not always so clear, this experiential learning; think of something Hud and Socrates might have shared though – this patience with knowledge. Hud relied on the teachings and promise of monotheism; Socrates relied on himself and Athens. Socrates had this saying – "Know thyself" – and if you keep questioning and answering, you'll find some (a?) ground for your actions.

Both men knew and didn't know. Hud knew of God's promise, the covenant of circumcision, and didn't know God's plans in this world, so to speak, so he waited. He waited like Noah waited five generations earlier. They both waited for God to act and they showed patience toward knowledge. Socrates knew of a method – a way of thinking – and he showed patience also.

This knowing and not knowing can be confusing. Take our Revolutionary War and all the differing views on it. One can imagine neighbors, kin, and congregations being split on the idea of revolting against their King and country. The colonists voted and, like almost all counting of votes, some people lost. Imagine how that must have felt and it puts winning or losing in 2004 in perspective.

Knowing and not knowing get all bound together. Last time any of us talked about this at any great length, life seemed pretty clear: mostly, everything changes as we age and a few things are certain – like age. The not knowing shows up with, well, stuff we don't know about. This is where it gets sticky. Sometimes the circle is divided into parts; in one part of the circle, no one claims to know what happens after death and in another part some claim the promise of monotheism and the guarantee of a day of Judgement.

Socrates drank the hemlock and met his end. We are told he could have taken banishment, but he chose otherwise, as Plato recorded Socrates' last words: *"The hour of departure has arrived, and we go our ways – I to die, and you to live. Which is better God only knows."* Socrates could have escaped his immediate death, but not death in general, by accepting banishment. Unlike the crucifixion of Jesus or the death of other prophets, Socrates was given a final choice; but, we are also told, in his 70 years of living, that he had only left Athens for military service and to visit the temple at Delphi. He had no place to go, so to speak, no place he wanted to be other than Athens. Like one of those old farmers who really can't live in a city, or like the character in *The Shawshank Redemption* – the one with the mouse who couldn't make it once he was paroled. It's like that sometimes, where leaving really isn't much of an option. It was that way to Socrates. He and Hud both accepted what happened, to a degree, and, *"which is better God only knows."*

13

Hud's monotheism was patient, as measured by his actions. Today all parts of monotheism are contested. The current series of warfare has a religious – that is, monotheistic – element. I won't argue that monotheism is the cause, but in war, making the enemy different is important. Purely as a thought game, if Iraq were 90% Christian Arab, it would be different – with or without oil. So religion is a factor – just how much, no one can say for sure.

Let's say Hud measured the world against God's promise. He waited in belief of God's knowledge. Today's situation is so much different. This period of warfare is grave, which just makes pain routine (and televised). The pain isn't always here, not here in the US, but in the state of world affairs. We could list them, but so could any time period; perhaps no worse than other times, even the time of Hud or Socrates, but the armies and weaponry have advanced. Warfare is more potent than ever, more potent than even 15 years ago. More potent than . . . imagine what it'll be in 50 years. We might want to consider other means of achieving political ends, given the rising costs, risks and demands of war.

What is the measure of things? For most of recorded time, humans thought the earth was the center of the universe. To them, it seemed, and one could argue rightfully so, that the universe was just something beautiful for the earth to look at. This changed over time, but can be captured in a moment of transformation – of regeneration – through the work of Copernicus; he taught that the earth revolved around the sun, the aptly named heliocentric theory. That must have been a big change for humans, to have theory and science combine to form knowledge – to decenter the earth – and to see it made so.

To the prophets of monotheism, the world of Copernicus, the world of 1514 – when he first proposed his wacky theory – and the world of 1543, when *De revolutionibus orbium coelestium*, or, *On the Revolutions of the Heavenly Spheres*, was published, it would have been a strange place indeed. After Copernicus, who dedicated his book to Pope Paul III, the earth was never again the center of anything, except what it had always been the center of: human perspective. We are the only ones who care about this stuff.

Consciousness is synaptic. It is the activity of sense and chemical. How the body perceives itself – how it sees itself – in its environment – that has an impact on thought. Thinking the world was flat had an impact; thinking that the world – or your part of it – thinking it is the center of it all, well, that has an impact too, and it takes a certain kind of brain, *a certain kind of ego*, to think that way. For example, does anyone still think the world is flat?

And think of the brain in general, anyone's brain. Why is there sometimes "noise" in the brain? Why does an active brain sometimes feel like a loud brain, and why also a quiet brain, a calm – like water – brain? Recall that Abraham heard Yahweh and the angels; recall that the Pythia made sounds, that is, verse, for Apollo. *It's sound, isn't it?* Hearing our thoughts, the self-reflexiveness, is a human quality; it's also how we relate to animals – our anthropomorphism. We see ourselves in our pets; we "see" them thinking and "hear" their thoughts. We communicate with pets, although it lacks depth let's say. We can't ask them about politics, sports, or what's on sale, but they do let us know things – like welcome home and something's going on out there. Pets.

14

"Riders on the storm," that's what this feels like – or more like, *"Writers on the storm."* I respect those who didn't write down their thoughts – non-writers like Abraham, Socrates, Jesus and the many others. The writers – they brought us the codes. Like most things, that's been good and bad.

In teaching pre-algebra, students have to learn certain skills. They are preparing for algebra, a skill and a way of thinking that has proven beneficial to us. The students I worked with often struggled with certain skills – fractions, integers and story problems, for example, that sort of math. They were usually ninth graders and they were frustrated. It wasn't that the students couldn't learn or hadn't tried; what had happened mattered less than the fact that they had begun to take it personally. When a student tries and fails, repeatedly, just like when it happens to adults, it takes its toll. Knowing that, I would try to break learning down, break it into smaller, useful, chunks. As teachers, we were trained and encouraged to use "manipulatives." These are hands-on teaching techniques to make math real (hand-held). To teach integers – positive and negative numbers – we would use a regular deck of cards. There would be 13 each of hearts, diamonds, spades and clubs. I always found the students to be familiar with cards, thus they were at ease and that gets them ready to learn.

Face cards in the deck all counted as 10. Aces were 1. Red cards were negative (an ace of hearts would equal – 1) and black cards were positive (an ace of clubs would equal 1). There would be five or six students around a small table; I would usually deal, and we would go through an exercise called "The Cards." At the beginning of the semester, this would be a card counting exercise, but once they got the hang of it, we could add lots of variations. The card counting exercise – the students called it a game – would start with a full deck of 52 cards, shuffled, with one card turned up in front of a student. Let's say an 8 of clubs came up: that would be +8. Then, to the next player or randomly, I would deal another card. Let's say it was a 10 of diamonds: that would be a – 10. So $8 - 10 = -2$. The student with the second card (the – 10) would respond and on we would go. If he or she was correct, I would deal another card to another student. If the answer had been incorrect, I would have analyzed the answer to see where the erring occurred. As a teacher, the direct action of the students, when they show you their thinking, that's when you can break it down, take it apart, and say something like, *"How's that?"* Having them participating and thinking – that's some good learning. It's great to see it take place, both in the immediate and over time.

Sometimes the number would climb high into the positives with a series of black cards (5+6+10+3+5+10+1 . . .); sometimes the opposite would happen and the number would climb high in a negative way (-5-3-4-1-10-10-7 . . .). Over time the students' accuracy and speed would increase in measurable ways. No matter the sequence, if we did our math correctly, the summation of 52 positive and negative cards is zero. (For every +3, for example, there would also be a –3: if done correctly, the count will always return to zero.)

In learning negative numbers, it wasn't always intuitive. I think as adults we all understand how debt accumulates – it grows. To lots of pre-algebra students, this is a new and difficult concept to master; once they get the idea, much of their math problems go away. It's like a piece of knowledge comes into being – they learn it – and they know what we mean. They can think differently, in negative and positive numbers, and it boosts their knowledge.

In visualizing negative numbers, we would use the idea of diving or cave exploring. With diving, I would tell them to imagine being 20 feet underwater (-20) and their diving instructor told them to come up 5 feet (+5): the new depth would be -15. We'd visualize that way, or with rappelling (going up and down) in a vertical cave.

Thinking in negative ways isn't negative thinking. It adds depth and perspective, and is required for various educational pursuits. It's a good model for the Is, this negative yet positive thinking.

15

Human emotions are independent of monotheism.

Many Americans are TV-watching, sugar-eating, God-fearing folks. They want Osama bin Laden killed. They want Saddam tried and executed. In the happening of events, they see God's hand in it.

After Mary was visited and made pregnant – impregnated – by the Holy Ghost, she went to visit Zechariah and Elizabeth in a city in Judah. At the time, Elizabeth was six months pregnant with John, soon to be known in history as John the Baptist. In Luke 1:41, we are told that Elizabeth felt the Holy Ghost when Mary and her fetus (Jesus) entered the room, and that fetus John the Baptist was said to have jumped.

Prophecy was not invented by any one clan or tribe, as it is found in all civilizations, to greater or lesser extent. Even in the time of Abraham, prophecy and prophets were well entwined into the fabric of political life.

There are many ways to interpret the development of monotheism as an idea. It seems almost universal that gods developed in all cultures, as humans used the gods to explain and order an ever-changing horizon. Out of knowledge we enter relationships with animate and inanimate objects. In a sense, we animate objects, that is, we give them meanings, to make our surroundings our own.

The stories told in mythology involve issues of death, regeneration, birth, rape, more death, war, sport, and in general, all aspects of human activity. We know that art and society are never held distinct, as neither are other aspects such as war and economics. Out of this, out of the swirling mix of human invention, come the prophets. One such emergence, a non-monotheistic example, was in Mari at about 2000 BC. Mari was a kingdom that bordered the Euphrates and today would have encompassed much of Syria and parts of Iraq. It seems the prophets of the fertility god Dagan spoke to the king and told him what it was Dagan wanted the king to know.

Where monotheism came from, whether from the prophets or from the people, is one of those questions scholars look for in the historical record. Famous scholars have spent their lives working on that question alone, though searches for beginnings tend to leave humans wondering. For example, Bible scholar Julius Wellhausen (1844-1918) argued that the prophets created "ethical monotheism." His point is contested. Yehezkel Kaufmann (1889-1963), author of *The History of the Religion of Israel*, argued against the idea that the prophets developed monotheism; instead, he and many others, hold the idea that ethical monotheism grew intuitively out of the people of Israel.

Ethical monotheism asserts one God and one morality, a whimsical idea to some, but one with the force of history. Some propose that prior to ethical monotheism people worshipped Nature, but this isn't the case. People worship power, simply put, and people were amazed and filled with wonder by Nature. But Nature, as a capital concept, has preceded God in death – ethical monotheism is a skeletal concept – a gasp at trying to tame the shrew (I don't think it's the last).

If morality was a natural fit to humans, if morality involved the "survival of the fittest," then the *most fit* would be somewhere between Abraham and anyone else. That is because there isn't any foundational experience humans can build upon that will last. When you look at the age of the planet, where we are situated in the universe, all the science that has changed our conception and understanding of the heavens, time and space, and then to build a life of faith around the musings of a tribal leader who at the age of 99 circumcised himself in the name of his God – what is there in that story that sparked a revolution? From the humble beginnings of God communicating with one human to our modern times with daily bombings in the Middle East and walls being constructed in land called holy, what is it that propels the old story upon us? What feeds monotheism and its ways?

Is it the claim to knowledge that is unknowable? Monotheism itself is based on Nature while denying that Nature is the substance of all things. Genesis opens with: *"In the beginning, God created the heavens and the earth."* The ordering is time first, then God, and then matter. *"In the beginning"* points to a time before time; *"God created"* points to an actor, a creator, with the skill to create *"the heavens and the earth"* (matter). But for many this dialectical arrangement is untenable. For example, some ask why are the heavens and the earth separated at the beginning? *"Why?"* questions usually don't fair well because they are predicated on answers that involve motives. The question: "Why did God suddenly want to create the heavens and the earth?" is unasked and unanswered. It is almost a whim of sorts, this God's workshop scenario. One could imagine God alone at his workbench of time. The God of monotheism has angels but doesn't work with a pantheon of gods. That would have mirrored the role of other systems, other religions, even the role of Nature with its winds and seasons; as a kid one of them was called *Old Man Winter*. We like naming things, which is a very human trait.

16

Don't be a hater – that's what some of my students taught me.

The 2004 elections were yesterday, and today there were no riots. That's right, the election process worked by channeling force: it works better than fighting it out in the streets. As we know, that's how it used to be done: the old *might makes right* idea. Voting is one of those social conventions, one of those virtues, which grew out of force. We can even see an example in the news, as you see the same thing happening – force precedes voting – in both Afghanistan and Iraq.

I made the claim earlier that the Is must be approached this way – as a premise and not a promise – as a means to discussion. I also said to keep the idea of a circle in mind, one you can enter from any direction and at any point.

How does your day begin? It's regular but not the same. That's part of what we are up to; the omphalos keeps moving – movement is constant. It comes from anywhere too, not just from the likes of Socrates, Copernicus and Nietzsche; it's found with the prophets also. Hmm, this ever-changing and unchanging world of ours.

The Is is going to go forward in this manner, with its focal point a countervalue to monothinking in whatever form it takes. In this chapter it has been the one God; in chapters two through four, the monothinking will be on messiahs, constitutions, and bodies. Let me just say again, that the Is is not against God, Allah, or monotheism. The Is isn't against messiahs, constitutions, or bodies. The Is is *both for and against* in the same way –1 holds 1 in place – a place where ideas become ideal. This is only a book, a collection of essays and aphorisms – something like "sticks and stones may break your bones, but words" . . . well, you remember the rest.

We are going to go further in each chapter – further with a pioneering spirit. We have to see how monothinking plays out politically. How do ideas work in the field? In the stories of the prophets we see *synoptic relationships* – similar ideas over differing times and yet familiar stories. There are also *synaptic relationships* – similar thoughts over differing times and yet familiar feelings. These are sense~chemical relationships. But this all has no meaning if there is no impact. Like beauty, what the Is does is have an impact.

There was a second Greek god at Delphi: Dionysus, the god of wine, resided there three months out of the year. Recall that Apollo's power was a gas – ethylene gas – and then he lets the god of wine – the god of intoxication – use his house, so to speak, and we again have a dramatic change in the sense~chemical combo taking place. Gas and wine – getting high – right at the birth of . . . a way of thinking, let's call it that – like algebra.

Abraham's way of thinking created a revolution; it is respected for its encapsulating assuredness. Copernicus comes to mind, as well as the others. And Socrates had a spirit that he listened to in his head – that's right – and he called it his *daimon*. He also had encapsulating assuredness; so does a circle.

See it? See how, in your mind, if we think it through, every thought can be in the circle, and every thought can be out of it. Once human's got/made consciousness, however that happened, we started thinking. We haven't stopped since. But there are different ways of thinking. People do think differently.

This isn't cultural – as in multicultural – this is human thought; multithought is accurate. We're the ones making all this happen. We're the culture-makers. Watch this country of ours come to life in the morning as the people go off to work. Off we go, day after day, making everything work in a way, for better and worse, humans doing what we do.

Monotheism is dead and it isn't dead, of course. It is alive and voting all over the world, and that's part of the Is. Take it for what it is, embrace, and dance. *Dance* you say? Yes. Find your spirit like a Socrates, or have faith in the God of monotheism, or find . . .

Yes, you know, you know more than you think: on to more beginnings.

2

Monotheism
(Or, What to do when a religion doesn't respect its messiah)

1

There is a move toward extinction. All around us things are "becoming" extinct, naturally, which means they are becoming nothing. We are Darwin's natural selectors when we place things on endangered lists. The extinct have only a past because their future is only in history. Birds are the first to go, or at least the first ones we miss. Our war on the peoples of the New World, that world that Columbus happened upon while looking for India, never had a chance. A few survive, but only a few. A friend of mine is working on Native American languages. He's working with the language of the Mandan, the aborigine tribe that helped Lewis and Clark survive the winter in the northern plains. There is one speaker left.

Do not be surprised to see monotheism here, as it provides us a beginning. We will use it to take a pioneering spirit to the teaching/message of Jesus, but not in the usual way. The Is will take anything of experience, and millions experience Jesus. So he's in. Now, by being in, he is also open to all forms of discussion.

2

11 September 2001: President George W. Bush, speaking to the nation after the bombings: *"Freedom was attacked today by faceless cowards, and freedom will be defended."*

In a day that went from terrorist acts to acts of war, it was a day of great escalation. This has been going on for some time now. On our part, our international policies in general, and specifically, the Shah of Iran, Lebanon, support for Saddam against Iran, support for the muhajadeen in Afghanistan until the Soviet military was defeated, the downing of an Iranian passenger jet in the Persian Gulf by our Navy, the troops in Saudi Arabia, the war in Iraq, and our support of Israel.

On their part, the bombings in general, and specifically, the 1983 killing of 241 US Marines in Lebanon, World Trade Center in 1993, Khobar Towers in 1996, our embassies in Kenya and Tanzania in 1998, the USS Cole, the destruction of the World Trade Center, the deaths in Pennsylvania, and the hole in the Pentagon.

Our president named it a war on terror.

America is well prepared for random acts of violence and dramatic events. We see them everyway, 24-7-365 $1/4$. We recover quickly from passions, moving from this to that, and that to this, thinking as long as it appears good it must be so. The war on terror is like that. It is without time, and it happens here, there and everywhere. It is a fact of war that a good enemy always looks different. When President Bush spoke, he called the enemy a faceless coward. By evening, the enemy had a face and the acts of terror (war) remained. These darn words, for we want to call them cowards, but cowardly acts cannot be so resolute – poor Bill Mahar and his politically incorrectness. The war on terror, as all wars do, involves ideological and economic stakes. When a country unites around a heinous act, they can be molded or mobilized for anything. September 11th has already been associated with Pearl Harbor enough for the reference to stick. It's worth noting that what began at Pearl Harbor ended at Nagasaki.

People from all walks of life, from the citizen on the street to President Bush, have said the terrorists attacked our freedom. What does that mean? Perhaps the only freedom we've lost, other than the current security adjustments, is the freedom to *make* the news: we're no longer the only main player. The war was televised, as we knew it would be. The world watched as the towers imploded and the Pentagon burned; and they watched as Bush hinted of war – a war on terror. This will last a very long time. How will we declare victory? And besides, only an idealist could imagine an end to terror; terror is war by another name, and it is part of us. Terror is to war what collateral damage is to killing the innocent: a euphemism. Here's the logic; a terrorist kills and a soldier causes collateral damage . . . dead is dead though, and, as we'll see below, perhaps we shouldn't put a premium on killing.

3

President Bush could make a good warrior, perhaps even a great one. His 2001, Yankee Stadium, World Series, in the middle of a National Terrorist Alert performance was flawless. He threw a perfect strike. He has been able to present a strong sense, if not presence, of toughness. He's good at saying things like: "This is a war of good vs. evil, and good will prevail."

If we want to protect America, in the immediate and in the future, we should be reminded of a fundamental rule of war: *guard against underestimating your adversary.* They believed enough in their cause to get 19 men to train and complete a complicated plan within enemy territory. They did their destruction while living among us and with our own technology.

We need to have a long discussion about what it is that "they" (there are many "theys" really – what Saudi Arabia needs isn't what Osama needs and so on) are demanding and what it is America needs to be secure. We need more than Senator Kerry and President Bush saying things like, "I'll kill the terrorists wherever . . ." and that kind of talk. That's good, but we need more than that. They are a dangerous and motivated enemy. They are not crazy. As witnessed, they are capable of hitting us hard. We shouldn't fear that, but we should respect the threat. I know, we witness heinous acts, acts right out of hell, and we want to do something. We want to strike back, even if, as a good friend of mine has said, it's reckless and with abandon: kill them as they kill us. The feel of the Old Testament lives on, with no one suggesting we turn the other cheek. That's okay, really, but from a born-again Christian president, it doesn't make any sense. Where's the forgiveness, right? I suppose if he were an atheist things would really be out of control.

4

War has always involved killing, but not on the magnitude and duration we are facing. There's a book called *The Art of War*. It was written around 400 BC by Sun Tzu, a writer from what we now call China. As you'll recall, this was also the time Pericles, Aspasia, Socrates, and the Greeks were active and the prophets were preaching. War, as a human invention, is subject to the same forms of change as everything else. We learn from the introduction to Sun Tzu's book that great changes began around 500 BC in China. War went from a seasonal activity – winter and summer were non-war periods because of the temperature – to a year round affair. Armies began conscripting peasants and *elite* (shock) troops were developed. The powerful crossbow was invented and deployed, making the use of the chariot extinct. The crossbow could be used with deadly force against the chariot – a couple of solid defeats and the human adapts. The development of a constant threat, new forces, and new technology, made the science of tactics all the more imperative.

Sun Tzu has gained a large following in the reading circles of military officers. They are a reading bunch, believe it or not. Some of the best thinking is found in military history books. Not only the impact of geopolitical thinking – from the likes of Machiavelli and Clausewitz – but, for example, the books about Erwin Rommel's campaigns in North Africa and Robert E. Lee's in Virginia, Maryland, and Pennsylvania, these are all studied and debated by military professionals. War is scientific, to a degree.

Sun Tzu presents war as art: his art was a science of tactics. Two forces are always at work. You are advised to engage the enemy through *cheng*, or orthodox, force, and also through *ch'i* – defined as unorthodox, unique, rare, or wonderful – force or forces. Think of a champion boxer who sets them up with a traditional force – jabs – and then comes around with something special – the knockout – and that's what Sun Tzu had in mind. Engage in an orthodox manner, and then surprise them with something. This required the military to have a lot of discipline. Commanders or soldiers who retreated in battle without orders were regularly beheaded. Even more to the point of discipline, there is a story from this time of an officer who went out to fight one of those champion battles: you know, when opposing champions would face each other before the armies themselves – an individual show of force. Well, at this time, many commanders were forbidding the practice, but the tradition persisted. One officer went off to battle and beheaded two enemy champions. When he returned from his victory, his own commander ordered him beheaded. An aide came to the champion's defense, but the commander replied: "Yes, I am confident he is an officer of talent, but he is disobedient." The officer was beheaded; the lesson of the tale is that even the highest values – a champion's victory – can be transvalued.

Sun Tzu's book is a collection of tactics on how to win a war. In part III, Offensive Strategy, there are 33 recommendations he makes. Number one is: *"Generally in war the best policy is to take a state intact: to ruin it is inferior to this. Do not put a premium on killing."*

His teachings suggest that the best tactics are the ones designed to make it easy to win. Breaking an enemy down, weakening the enemy's will to resist, that is the best approach. Actual combat should be short, the least possible cost in lives and resources, and inflict the *fewest* possible enemy casualties.

Why the "fewest" possible enemy casualties? According to Sun Tzu, you want few enemy casualties because you have to think of the future and the time of government. War is a political weapon to be used sparingly, and then only when the path to victory has been well prepared.

5

The more than 3,000 dead, four downed planes, two destroyed towers, and the attack on the Pentagon, changed our thoughts. The *"What Would Jesus Do?"* bracelets and logos disappeared. I mean, it is fair to ask – What would Jesus do? In his life he never led armies, so there's no evidence he would counsel bombings or invasions, and yet Christian evangelicals turned out with *morals in voting hand*, supported the president's policies, and carried him to reelection. To some, it must look like America turns the other cheek only in order to get a good wind-up. We turn the other cheek all right, just to get a better swing. We are tough. Look at what we've done since, what, Jamestown, Virginia, the first permanent colony in 1607; from a fort on a peninsula to a leading world power in 400 years – incredible really.

The worst recorded day of death in US history is not 11 September 2001. On 17 September 1862, near Sharpsburg, Maryland and a stream called Antietam, more than 23,000 American citizens were wounded or killed in our Civil War. Due to the medical care of the time, and the types of wounds inflicted, the National Parks Service conservatively estimates that 7,640 died.

On 7 February 1945, American and British bombers dropped incendiary bombs on the German city of Dresden. The raid created a firestorm that killed 35,000 people and destroyed more than 80% of the city. World War II ended in Europe a little over two months later. Today's war is fought symbolically. If 9/11 is the new Pearl Harbor, what event will be the new Hiroshima and/or Nagasaki? Or maybe a Dresden will do?

The Old Testament, as many of you know, has a story about an eye for an eye: someone hits you and you are justified in hitting 'em back. It works in a similar manner in Islamic countries. For example, in Saudi Arabia they cut off the hand of a thief.

Now imagine for a moment our 100 US Senators. Instead of calling for a New Testament response to the attack, as we'll discuss below, we get a call of death to those who did this. Any counsel of patience, the patience of Hud, for example, fails to appear. Even if it did it would have most likely been ridiculed into silence. What politician will ask for patience? In fact, we often don't understand patience because we don't understand how others see us. We've gotten full of ourselves and our hype … so much so that the obesity isn't just around our waist.

All war books preach that you must always know your enemy. We can begin to understand this enemy by looking at the targets they selected. They targeted people and symbols. They targeted our citizens, the World Trade Center towers, a vital part of our economy, and the Pentagon, a symbol of our military establishment. The fourth target was surely also vital and symbolic; we are told it was the White House. These targets are war targets. That said, a "war on terror" is a war by another name. It really is a war, and should be properly named. (In fact, can we win a misnamed war?) But calling it a war on terror is misleading – much like the misnamed war on drugs. America, the home of the pharmaceutical industry, will never be drug-free; the United States, founded in war, will never be free of war. We will also never be free of terrorism. Remember Timothy McVeigh, the Desert Storm veteran who was awarded the Bronze Star? We created him; I don't like it, but it's true. We can lay the blame somewhere else if we like, but the Is can take it in. That's one of the issues with the truth – we don't always like what we hear.

6

Christianity gave us the book of Romans, Paul's letter to the newly formed Christian sect living in a great empire. In Romans 2:1, Paul said this about judging others: *"You, therefore, have no excuse, you who pass judgement on someone else, for at whatever point you judge the other, you are condemning yourself, because you who pass judgement do the same things."*

That kind of message is a lot different than the Old Testament, and it is revolutionary writing. To say that you should not judge is traditional: remember how Hud told the disbelievers of their wrongs, but he waited for God to act. The same is found in what Paul is saying. In some ways, what I'm beginning to wonder, is what it means to say the US is a Christian nation, when it doesn't seem to follow key Christian themes. When people say they believe in God, I'm beginning to see an America that means the Old Testament God. That would make America closer to the Jewish and Muslim faith than I ever really thought. Plainly, in a New Testament way, the love and forgiveness of the peace child was absent when President Bush declared war. Somehow, it seems, war justifies itself. We're "at war" so the resurrection can be forgotten. What of Paul's words in Romans 12:19? *"Do not take revenge, my friends, but leave room for God's wrath, for it is written: 'It is mine to avenge; I will repay, says the Lord'."* That too can be forgotten. It might be of interest to note that Leo Tolstoy, the Russian novelist of *War and Peace*, used Romans 12:19 to perfection in *Anna Karenina*; he uses the line to preface the book and the whole book, considered his greatest, is found in that verse.

Paul, in writing about Jesus' message, often brought the Old Testament into what would be called the New Testament. For example, Romans 12:19 is taken from Deuteronomy 32:35. Christians tend to go back to the Old Testament for guidance, but Jesus' disciples did that already. The old is part of the new, that's the point, just like a change of command ceremony.

Many ask: *"Do we do the same things as the terrorists?"* No. America does not fly hijacked passenger jets into skyscrapers and military headquarters. We do kill civilians in the context of military action and we do bomb military headquarters; our last declared war, World War II, ended with the atomic bombings of Imperial Japan's cities, Hiroshima and Nagasaki. Today, we think of them as justified war targets: others may call them something else. So our actions speak to others differently than they do to us. To others, the death and destruction has grown to be too much. The death of Iraqis, through insurgent bombs or our own, and we call it the price to be paid, by them, for freedom . . . and collateral damage is still a euphemism.

Who wonders how many Iranians died because of the Shah and our support of him? – Or how many Iranians died because we armed and supported Iraq? And then, how many Iraqis have died because after we supported Saddam against Iran, we turned away during the time to make peace? Really, it doesn't take much to imagine some bitterness. We like to think it's because of our freedom, though it's not; it's about power, and, ultimately, only the present can deal with the past and the future.

It is becoming clear to me that what is in the New Testament seems to have little to do with our international policies, but is it clear that this isn't necessary? I mean, Paul and the other writers of the New Testament did that already – they brought the old into the new. For example, take a look at Romans 3:9-18 and see the connections – see the bridges – and see the old *already in* the new:

> 9: What shall we conclude then? Are we any better? Not at all! We have
>   already made the charge that Jews and Gentiles alike are all under sin.
> 10: As it is written: "There is no one righteous, not even one;
> 11: there is no one who understands, no one who seeks God.
> 12: All have turned away, they have together become worthless;
>   there is no one who does good, not even one."
>   (Psalms 14:1-3; 53:1-3; Ecclesiastes 7:20)
> 13: "Their throats are open graves;
>   their tongues practice deceit." (Psalm 5:9)
>   "The poison of vipers is on their lips." (Psalm 140:3)
> 14: "Their mouths are full of cursing and bitterness." (Psalm 10:7)
> 15: "Their feet are swift to shed blood;
> 16: ruin and misery mark their ways,
> 17: and the way of peace they do not know." (Isaiah 59:7-8)
> 18: "There is no fear of God before their eyes." (Psalm 36:1)

Augustine, Martin Luther and John Wesley all traced their spiritual renewal to a reading of Romans. I'm not a Christian; I was born one, circumcised, baptized, and confirmed, but I lack their kind of faith (there are many kinds). I do believe in the message of love, and I don't believe it needs the resurrection. Also, I have faith, I trust in things; I trust this world and have faith that you can expect anything.

7

Controversy is (of course) part of a pioneering spirit, so I want to suggest that the disciples, and perhaps Jesus himself, misunderstood his message. Too often, his message has been codified in one way, and because of the effect of time, no one can see all the other messages. They, the disciples, placed the power of the peace child in the fulfillment of Old Testament prophecies. This is good, but there's more to it. It matters little if it was *foretold*; it matters more that it was *told*. The power of the peace child is the gift of love. The power isn't in the resurrection, the end of time, its power and gift is in the present. Now, not later.

16 September 2001: My mom's pastor told her that Christianity was about justice. What that does is binds Jesus' message of love with the story of his resurrection. But his message of love is independent of the act of resurrection. It's like saying because someone doesn't come back from the dead, then what they said isn't valued in a divine way. Funny how that is. Jesus may or may not have been resurrected, that isn't the question: his teaching – his way of thinking – that is one of his influences on consciousness. Preaching love matters and it changes humans. So does preaching hate – think anti-Semitism, anti-Arabism, anti-black, anti-gay, and . . . hate is strong in humans.

16 September 2001: Senator Hillary Rodham Clinton was talking on one of the Sunday morning news shows. When asked about the possibility of casualties in a ground war in Afghanistan, she said, "we've already had military casualties," referring to the dead and wounded in NYC, at the Pentagon, and in Pennsylvania. She concluded that casualties in a ground war were now acceptable in fighting terrorism. If that is so, then it is also reasonable to impose a peace on Israel and Palestine. If we are willing to risk casualties in the mountains of Afghanistan or the roads of Iraq, then why not get between the Palestinians and Israelis? Casualties? Yes. More than we've already suffered? Unknowable.

And let's not scoff at this point until we consider this: the conflict between the Palestinians and Israelis is a known thorn. What must be resolved is the question of Jerusalem, and specifically, the space known by two names: by Muslims as Haram al-Sharif and by Jews as the Temple Mount. They both claim it and they both believe in it (looks like we need a Solomon moment). On the other hand, ending the war on terror is factually impossible. It would be like ending war. It won't end. War can only be stifled, suppressed, but not killed. One would have to say it is a resilient emotion.

Here is the question about the influence of love: either the prophecy of the messiah was fulfilled or it wasn't? If it was, then where is the effect – where is the love? If there is no influence, than the religious bearing of America is more Jewish and Muslim – more Abrahamic – than I understood, for without faith in the peace child, Christianity is as hollow as Marxism is without faith in the proletariat.

16 September 2001: After returning from Camp David and meetings about the war on terror, President Bush said: *"We will rid the world of evil doers."* What am I to think of our president and his policy? Has he not read Romans 12:17-18?

> 17: Do not repay anyone evil for evil. Be careful to do what is right in the eyes of everybody.
> 18: If it is possible, as far as it depends on you, live at peace with everyone.

Or the next verse – Tolstoy's verse?

> 19: Do not take revenge, my friends, but leave room for God's wrath, for it is written: "It is mine to avenge; I will repay, says the Lord." (Deuteronomy 32:35)

Or verses 20-21, where we read Paul's words on how to treat an enemy and face an evil?

> 20: On the contrary: "If your enemy is hungry, feed him; if he is thirsty, give him something to drink. In doing this, you will heap burning coals on his head." (Proverbs 25:21-22)
> 21: Do not be overcome by evil, but overcome evil with good.

This isn't academic, as millions take these words to be sacred. You can't be for something and then go against it all the time. I mean, theoretically you can, and they have a word for it, but why? It's like reading the directions and then not following them, and we know how well that works. Or it's like being a Chicago Bears fan and then rooting for the Packers: what's the point? Christians hold the words in Romans to be special, not me. I happen to like the words myself and keep coming back to them in order to try to understand the present. But if Paul's words are holy, then, they are holy, right? With evangelical Christianity, you don't get to pick what's sacred, as it is already specified. Really, it would be like someone claiming to be an atheist and then praying five times a day to Allah. It would mean something, but not what was meant. This causes problems. Like a 2,000-year thinking-binge, getting over the hangover is going to take some time.

It's not about judging the followers of Abraham, not in the sense of you're wrong and I'm right – not at all. We share an interest in thinking about life and we share the fact that we have beliefs in the matter. It's about how we think, and it seems that the influence of peace is often missing in international relations. Reality is difficult and often even scary. The way life is often presented, well, Jim Morrison comes to mind: *"The future's uncertain and the end is always near."* With that sentiment and to that end, Christian thought wants to improve life's situation, and concepts like love, faith, and heaven give it meaning. As we know, these are celebrated at times like Christmas and Easter, and also at funerals. At other times, Christians display their faith by wearing crosses and symbols such as the *WWJD* bracelets. Christian thought is complex. In abortion they can be pro-life, but not always, and concerning forms of justice, they can be pro-death, but not always. If we think of what Paul says (that we are to feed an enemy and to give them water), there is non-judging built into the system, or at least compassion for basic human needs.

8

I've seen the evening news a couple of times this week. The military operations in Falluja are taking place. The reporters are embedded with the Marines. It's tough work there in Falluja. The house-to-house securing of a city of 300,000, with the embedded video and commentary from the Marines, while in action, taking fire, that's amazing. Imagine being at Gettysburg, or Antietam, or some other battle like that. I'll say this: the mission is too much, you could argue, as there is power in forbearance. I'm not interested in a rehashing of how/why we are where we are geopolitically. Iraq, Afghanistan, September 11th, and all the bombings and conniving before, they are all past. But remember our troops and what we are asking of them. We are their employer: we pay them to do our bidding. I know, I took the money awhile. It's not like anyone coerced me – I wasn't drafted. No one made me join the Reserve Officer Training Corp (ROTC) or volunteer to go to Saudi Arabia: nope, no one but me.

But hey now, what is it we were after? The mission, that's right. There's no one-way to fight terror, as there are many ways to do it. One is to create enemies, and one is to not create enemies. There will always be opposition; there doesn't always have to be enemies, and that makes a difference.

Right after World War II and before the Cold War got going, the Department of War became the Department of Defense (DOD). This was accomplished by the 1947 National Security Act (NSA), which brought the War and Navy departments under one rubric and created the US Air Force out of the Army Air Corps. The NSA also reformed the wartime Office of Strategic Services into the Central Intelligence Agency and created the executively controlled National Security Council. The NSA, Truman Doctrine and Marshall Plan were the major components of the Cold War's policy of containment.

We changed the name of the Department of War because of a new perceived threat, that of communism. Since then Congress has stopped declaring war, which abdicates the power of *We the People* to declare war to the commander-in-chief. It appears that as long as we called it a defensive operation – containment – we didn't have to call it a real war – it was a "Cold War." Now with offensive operations, the word war is back in vogue; we'll see if the Constitution comes back as well.

The enactment of the NSA created a unified military command. Prior to this, the Army and Navy ruled: the Army controlled the Department of War and the Navy had the Department of the Navy. With the growth in military power after WW II, to include the new technologies of war, such as jet planes and hydrogen bombs, the US thought it needed a new organization. At first, from 1947 until 1949, the three department heads (Army, Navy, Air Force) maintained a degree of institutional independence. In 1949 the NSA was amended to streamline their subordination to the Secretary of Defense. Given today's international realities (WW III perhaps?) it's time to once again rename the DOD. There appear to be two alternatives. One is to go back to the original name since the policy of containment served its role and has recently been abandoned by President

Bush's policy of preemption. The DOD should either be renamed the Department of War, or a new name more inline with Bush's policies – perhaps the Department of Offense, the DOO, would work? The DOO would be based on technology and preemption, so not much will change. What does change is the added emphasis on the offensive attainment of political ends. We've learned over time that offensive bombs kill just as well as defensive ones.

9

I said earlier that one could either create or not create enemies. Think of it like someone at work who is always meddlesome or always individualistic. Both ways can lead to relationship problems. It seems to be the same with international relations. There is a possibility, it becomes routine, and then falls into habit. Sometimes this is for the best, other times it isn't. That's where thinking comes in, both the reasonable and unreasonable. If we ask a motive question – *Why?* – and seek some answers, we'll come up with some. We won't know how good they are until we test them with experience, but it is a place to start. Sometimes we answer why questions with faith. Faith, a particular kind of faith, has taken over many types of thinking. For example, it has, in general, replaced forbearance as a common quality.

How would we go about not creating enemies? That does seem to be the point at the moment. It appears that enemies are created when we get into other people's stuff. Really, that's about it. Call it engagement or interference, whichever partisan side you are on, but there is something hazardous about humans coming together. Invariably, violence breaks out. Not always, of course, but it does. No real answer to why violence or nonviolence breaks out, as that points to meaning. What we are after is what Is. Violence is – what it means is up to us.

Humans have a habit of holding on to principles. This is a good quality, cherished even, but it also can be debilitating. We sometimes hold on to them too long in the face of change. In military terms, the principle of valor found in the chariot charge was negated by the invention of the crossbow. It would have been foolish and disastrous to keep using chariots against crossbows. Intellectual principles without reasons are what Nietzsche referred to as faith; the principles themselves begin to suffice and not experience. Perhaps our Vietnam War is an American example of this. Faith in various high principles – stopping the spread of communism, for example – were more than enough to carry this country through years of warfare – often times with hundreds of military personnel killed *per day*. Faith in principles does not mean success. There's more to it than that. We need to look less at what our principles mean – things like freedom – and more to what it is they create. As they say, history is filled with good intentions gone badly.

10

What monotheism judges, the Is accepts: where monotheism promises good and evil, the Is premises good and bad. That means, in both cases, that everything humans have ever done – everything – Is. We may even call terrible things inhuman: what we mean is animal. We sometimes forget we are that too. When we start calling and naming things, we've already created value. The truth doesn't benefit anyone in particular. Those who hold on to the past and cherish custom, they believe the seekers of truth to be selfish. This is with merit, as they are (we all are). It is a harmless kind of selfishness though to the community or state at large. It will consume and pay taxes just as before, but absent some ill effects of . . . well, let's say absent effects of ill principles. Judging, we should not forget, is countered by non-judging.

11

Romans 7:21 – "*So I find this law at work: When I want to do good, evil is right there with me.*"

That's the issue with morals, the values that humans create – they keep showing up, don't they? Paul means all action is complicated. One person's patriot or freedom fighter is another person's rebel or insurgent. Paul knew it: that's why he tended toward peaceful resolutions and not war. Our question gets clearer – the one about respecting your messiah: what is missing from Jesus' message that war can be so readily accepted by his followers? How is a messenger of peace used by adherents to support the imposition of democracy and freedom through violent means (war)?

It is possible to attack people and say, "We bring you peace." I understand we used this approach on the aborigine – this is an American book – and it looks like we are going global now. Wouldn't you think a Jesus-inspired (based) international relations policy would focus on peaceful resolutions and not warfare? A Jesus-inspired policy might call for things like biannual peace conferences. Do we really think Prime Minister Tony Blair and President Bush, along with their staffs, do we really think we can't outthink an opposition? The dead, if they could, they would demand that we try. I mean, think of the troops and what we ask them to risk, and then think what Paul and Sun Tzu might have counseled, and you begin to see a different analysis enter your thoughts: we think quickly of war and not so quickly of peace.

That's a good combination – Paul and Sun Tzu – the peace preacher and the artist of war. Recall Sun Tzu's first maxim on Offensive Strategy: one shouldn't put a premium on killing. Unless Paul is a total pacifist (not likely), Sun Tzu's counsel might be something he would consider, well, reasonable.

12

Americans are seekers of meaning and not of what Is. Pursuing meaning (however defined) they find it doesn't last. The senses dull, age takes over, and we become habits. Our senses have been made dull by use. Perhaps it is the waiting, the waiting in faith, which has dulled the peace sense in America's form of Christianity (there are over 600 denominations in the US). It was dull with me, dull enough that I joined the Army and learned about war. It felt good to serve. The Army helped me in lots of ways. It honed my senses and helped me over some fears. If I summed up my Army experiences, I would call them good.

War adds meaning to life in ways peace doesn't (and *vice versa*). The sense of death, how it feels to humans and its meaning, has an advantage of time over peace. Death's impact is immediate and lasting; the impact from peace is mediated and fleeting. I wonder if that is part of the problem – the impact of each. Remember that Jesus said he would return. The disciples thought so and didn't think it would take this long. Christians keep his return as an article of faith. The farmers I grew up around – Christians mind you – well, they had this phrase about Jesus and his return. They'd see something slow – like someone running slow to first base during a ball game – and they'd say he was: "*slower than the second coming of Christ.*" I didn't get it much then, but the quip is interesting. Maybe this is one of those dilemmas, this waiting for his return and the day of Judgement, which lead or bridge to meaning limited by a past, present or future, and not the Is. The Is, simply put, is a bridging mechanism to human value. Whatever we do, we do; meaning comes next. We'd do better by thinking through our options and possibilities rather than our limits.

In Sun Tzu's section on Offensive Strategy, he uses experience as a teacher and points to five circumstances in which victory may be predicted. The way to victory is:

- by knowing when to fight and when not to;
- by understanding the use of both large and small forces;
- when your ranks are united in purpose;
- when you are prudent and your enemy is not;
- and when generals are not interfered with.

Notice how victory is a thing within human influence. That's important.

13

We treat politics like the weather: something to talk about but something we can't do anything about. We treat it like a happening and not an act. Energy wasted on objects, be it flag-flying or flag-burning, the Wailing Wall or the Haram al-Sharif, the World Trade Center or the mountains of Afghanistan, all point to *non-relationships*; we are discussing *things* and not *the relationships people have to them*. This is important. When people are reduced to things, we get phrases like collateral damage. To wit, if the World Trade Center had been empty on September 11th, it would have made a difference. Losing empty buildings is no big symbolic loss. Who cares? What matters from September 11th is the loss of life. Reducing death to collateral damage, one seemingly has little thought of another's life, be they friend or foe.

Tens of thousands died in Hiroshima and Nagasaki moments – remember those? – and we called it victory and won a war. Or this: from 28 September 2000 to 5 October 2001, 670 Palestinians and 182 Israelis died in their war. You see, we talk often of things, of objects, and not people and their relationships. A dead New Yorker, a dead Afghani, a dead Iraqi, and a dead anyone: the body dies and the relationship is missed, be it father, mother, child, sibling, lover or mate. The God of monotheism told Moses, "*Thou shalt not kill.*" It doesn't get much clearer than that: commandment #6. God didn't say Thou shalt not kill unless the accused has had a fair trial; or Thou shalt not kill unless you really think it will do some good; or Thou shalt not kill unless you feel threatened. Thou shalt not kill: this isn't Animal Farm.

14

I joined the US Army through ROTC at the University of Illinois and was commissioned a 2nd Lieutenant in 1986. My eight years as a supply (Quartermaster) officer were unexceptional; I served and most of it was reserve time. I was on active duty for training, plus a couple weeks in Germany and the five months in Saudi Arabia. Even though, during the 1980s, we were all trained to fight the Soviet Union and Eastern bloc countries, the Army prepares you for change. All soldiering is contingent on something else – the mission or other soldiers most often. Thus, with the end of the Cold War, I found myself volunteering for a tour in support of Desert Storm. I spent five months in Saudi Arabia after the conclusion of major conflict. At the time, July-November of 1991, Desert Storm was winding down and Iraq had been thrown out of Kuwait. Our mission was to process the Army out of the country and bring it home.

There were no bombings during my time in Saudi Arabia. We weren't even armed with M-16s or pistols. We were issued gas masks and had to carry them around in case Hussein lobbed some Scud missiles at us. While in country, for most of my time I lived in the Khobar Towers, a large housing complex just outside of Dhahran and the US airbase that was there. In one of those early signs of trouble, the Khobar Towers were truck-bombed in 1996. We lost 19 in that bombing.

War is part of the Is as "contested values" are political: there are alternatives. Possibility doesn't equal necessity though; if something is necessary, then the possible has already been contained. In the US we've made fear necessary. Our entertainment-news sources play on this. They are not wicked, the media, as they are only obeying the rules of the market, just like most of us do every day. The possible and capitalism go well together; they both know how to commodify, which generates supply and demand, scarcity and excess. It wasn't until capitalism slogged through the industrial age that it really began to hit its stride. Now and in the future technology will expand what the possible can mean, as well as what it Is.

15

So, what to do when a religion doesn't respect its messiah? Well, at this point, given Paul's words in Romans, the lack of respect does appear to be a defensible position. This isn't an indictment or conviction, mind you, but I would call it a point of contention.

If you remove Jesus-inspired ideas from Jesus' message, it does become odd, doesn't it? If there is no noticeable effect in international policy, but an effect in politics – the election – then perhaps we have come across something interesting. Jesus-inspired themes resonate in some political areas and not others. But wait? . . . Christian themes do show up in international policies in the form of family planning, abstinence, drug laws, AIDS, and lots of other issues. Hmm . . . We are still searching for a motive, a good reason, for negating Jesus-inspired themes from war making. The old policy of containment, as we discussed, was focused on "defense." And, as we know, this led to many defensive-offensive conflicts like Korea and Vietnam. Now with the US turning toward an offensive policy, now when you would think Jesus' message might make a strong appearance . . . we get instead, old-fashioned power politics.

From a New Testament/Paul perspective (or Sun Tzu) this doesn't look good. We have a strong appearance, strong effect, and misnamed or misplaced message. This indifference, this lack of respect for Jesus' main message – the one about peace – if it is fairing this poorly in a time of war, then there is a disconnect in the message and meaning. This isn't about hope because, while possible, there's no guarantee the situation will correct itself. If we wanted it to, as a nation – remember one key circumstance for victory is unity in the ranks – we could, but we don't have the words for it, at least we don't seem to be preparing the way for it. Instead, to confront with our military might, as we have done, we have placed a premium on killing. As Sun Tzu suggests, this makes victory harder to attain, but not impossible.

War is the most important state activity. The power to wage war is codified in the US Constitution and it was given to the people, to us. They could have designed the system differently, but they chose the people. If we do consider renaming the DOD, as we should, let's go with the title that got us through two world wars, the traditional title and concept, the Department of War. Naming a department by its strategy gives away too much information and, frankly, blinds our thinking. War, as the name of a department, means just that, while leaving the name of our actions – offense and defense – open to discussion. War is then the focus and not the strategy.

Also, respecting your messiah isn't such a bad way of putting it, even in warfare. The word means, outside of the Christian context we usually hear it in, it means "deliverer" or "liberator." Christians take this idea and apply Jesus to it, but others can use the idea of liberation found there – there's no monopoly on liberation either.

16

Well, with Jesus' message or without it, we still have to win this war we are in. But what does victory look like and how to prepare the way? Sun Tzu closes his chapter on Offensive Strategy with three maxims on victory – the last of 33:

> 31. Therefore I say: know the enemy and know yourself; in a hundred
>   battles you will never be in peril.

> 32. When you are ignorant of the enemy but know yourself, your chances
>   of winning or losing are equal.

> 33. If ignorant both of your enemy and of yourself, you are certain in
>   every battle to be in peril. – Such people are called "mad bandits."
>   What can they expect if not defeat?

Know the enemy and know yourself, and in a hundred battles . . . back to knowing. Socrates said know thyself: Sun Tzu said know the enemy and yourself. If the way to victory isn't prepared through Jesus' message of peace, then winning this war is knowing how to prepare the way to victory – and avoiding mad bandits.

3

Oligarchy
(Or, What to do with an unconstitutional spirit in the House of Representatives)

1

We were still at war with tribes when Illinois became a state in 1818. The last battle was 14 years later, in 1832, when a chief named Black Hawk and his tribes were chased north into the future Wisconsin (statehood 1848) and defeated by the banks of the Mississippi River at the Battle of Bad Ax. Black Hawk was captured and sent to Washington DC, where he was paraded as a defeated warrior. He was returned to Iowa, paid a pension by the government, and died in 1838.

Now, I'm not interested in throwing a pity-party for chief Black Hawk. I grew up on land that was his, you could say: a farm of 160 acres in Jo Daviess County, Illinois. On a map, the county is in the northwest corner of Illinois – the one that borders Iowa and Wisconsin at the Mississippi River. As a kid growing up there, I was aware that someone had lived here before; for example, we'd find arrowheads in the field after plowing, or just lying there along a river bed.

With Black Hawk, I just want you to see the beginning of something – how something takes on its own life. In 1673, seven French explorers led by Louis Joliet, a fur trader, and Jacques Marquette, a Jesuit missionary, traveled across the land west of Lake Michigan on a mission to find the river referred to as "Messipi." When they found it, they were to follow it to the sea. They traveled by river and portage, and with the help of the locals, they "found" the Mississippi River. They traveled down-river and made it as far as modern-day Arkansas. Here they learned from the local tribes that the Spanish controlled the river if they went any farther. The explorers turned back and traveled 240 miles across the prairie on the Illinois River. From a map perspective, they ended up just south of Lake Michigan by modern-day Joliet, Illinois. That had to be something. I mean, 1673, in the middle of nowhere, with a fur trader, a priest, five other guys, a few guns and a couple of canoes. Think of it – Jamestown, Virginia would have been 66 years old. That's a pioneering spirit.

There's a strange custom in America about not discussing religion and politics in mixed company, but, as we see, it's always been mixed company. All these things keep going on at the same time. I'm sure the aborigine didn't think much of seven men in a couple of canoes. Who would have thought that once seven arrived that they would tell a few, and then trading begins, along with the missionary work, and more traders come, and then settlements and forts. I doubt anyone imagined that seven French explorers signaled the end and I doubt anyone imagined that in 159 years, from the first encounter in 1673 to the last in 1832, that *all* the tribes would be gone from Illinois – a place named after the aborigine.

2

This chapter is on people and representation. Representative government is a human invention. America has been a leader in this idea and it is even what we proposed for the former Soviet states and are implementing in Afghanistan and Iraq. A "constitution" is also individual. We are constituted beings: there are things that make us who we are. The same is true of governments.

Prior to constitutions, kings and queens (monarchies) ruled. With the invention of constitutions, the people claimed a right to government. The writers and ratifiers of our Constitution treated it like *a map of right principles*. They were trying to tame power, to tame factionalism, by giving it time and space to present itself. They weren't trying to silence groups, but to give them a voice. That is the subtle genius that we have lost, but it's in there, in the Constitution, and we're going to see about using it.

I'll begin by telling you up front what this is about: it'll be revolutionary, though like it was in 1789, the revolution will be constitutional. Following the Constitution isn't an overturning of value; it is implementing an existing value. Revolution done by following our Constitution may not sound correct – call it re-formation if you prefer. Below, I'll go into depth on a couple of issues to show you what has happened to this power of ours. Again, with the Is, this isn't done out of morality, *per se*. We live under a constitution in the United States, and that of itself isn't that moral. Today, we know from experience that humans like to amass power, and this principle was well known to the founders and ratifiers of the Constitution. They knew that in order to counter this principle of power, to counter its effect, you had to balance power between interests. In our case, the compromise was a balance between states and the people. The framers could have designed and submitted for ratification a system that favored one set of interests over another, or even a Legislative Branch with one chamber (*unicameral*), but they didn't. They wanted a balanced system of checks and created and ratified a Legislative Branch with a House of Representatives, the people's House, and a Senate, the states' House. Nowadays we miss the significance of the separation. I missed it for decades. We've grown accustomed to looking down on people, to think they are not capable of things like self-government, but the ratifiers believed otherwise. They talked of the genius of the American people; they didn't find our genius in our superior intellect, but in our way of sorting out factionalism. They had just come out of a revolutionary/civil war, and they knew how bad things could get and what concepts like liberty and freedom and security meant. The genius of the people was found in allowing a representative of a group to vote another's interest. One representing many; the genius was in the concept, which meant trusting in the represented interests of others, not simply individuals, but an individual representing individuals (others). The genius is still there today.

What has evolved in the US House of Representatives was never the intent of the members of the Constitutional Convention; neither was it the will of the state governments that ratified the document. The delegates and ratifiers had a good understanding of humans. They also had a good understanding of why a people's House – one described in Federalist 55 by James Madison as a House: *"for the purposes of safety, of local information, and of diffusive sympathy with the whole society."* They understood why a people's House with its lofty standard would not necessarily protect the people: a high principle is hollow unless you can back it up. Backing it up meant providing a means for supporting them, the factions formed by the people, and to devise a way for them to express themselves. It is this principle that has been misplaced but not lost. The House, as an institution, was designed to be augmented – to grow – and if you do not augment something designed to be augmented, if you do not allow it to grow in response to its environment, then you change a fundamental element of a thing and it becomes something else. That is what has happened to the US House of Representatives. Our House isn't at all what it was intended to be: *it has become a place of the few instead of the many.*

3

Friedrich Hayek wrote a 1945 essay, "The Use of Knowledge in Society." In it is a reminder of why local information is the point of entry for all science, even the science of government. Science is not the sum of all knowledge: there are too many particulars for scientific knowledge to ever have a general rule. (That's why a circle, with parts coming and going, as something moving and changing, seems to be a good thought model for knowledge.) The knowledge anyone possesses has to be known, it has to be in that individual's so-called circle of knowledge; if it's not known – like how to make gunpowder or use a compass – then it is not available as knowledge.

This is useful for pointing to the importance, both theoretically and politically, of a large membership for the House of Representatives. It is the general population who has this knowledge of the particular: it is not found in the few, the oligarchy. It is the locals who know the circumstances of time and place. This theory is also found in *The Federalist Papers*. It is through the knowledge of local conditions that the House was to prosper and keep its balance – to be a counterweight to oligarchy, to rule by the few.

4

There is power in representation, and like all power, it is changeable. The power of the people at the federal level, or at a local level, can be changed. This gets into fractions and ratios, like some of the math from chapter one. Let's start by saying the fraction 1/30,000 is not equal to the fraction 1/647,000.

Our system of government places the people's power in a ratio. If we all voted on all the items, a strict democracy, the ratio would be 1/1. But you can see why that wouldn't work: too many voters and nothing would get done. On the other hand, you can see that a ratio that is disproportionate to the intent of the system, well, you could see how that might shift power to other groups and away from the people, from the citizens.

The idea that one can represent others, be it a group of 300, 3,000, 30,000, or 300,000, and you can see this is a concept we use today. The current ratio of Representative to represented in the US House is higher than it has ever been in our history. Today the ratio is one Representative for every 647,000 people. For reference, here is a list of the ratio's history – marked by census dates. You'll note that the ratio keeps increasing:

US House of Representatives: *Representative to Represented Ratio History*	
Year	**Rep/Represented**
1790	1/33,000
1800	1/36,000
1810	1/37,000
1820	1/44,000
1830	1/52,000
1840	1/75,000
1850	1/96,000
1860	1/119,000
1870	1/130,000
1880	1/154,000
1890	1/174,000
1900	1/193,000
1910	1/211,000
1920	1/242,000
1930	1/281,000
1940	1/301,000
1950	1/344,000
1960	1/410,000
1970	1/455,000
1980	1/519,000
1990	1/570,000
2000	1/647,000
2010	1/?

The ratifiers of the Constitution debated this concept in great detail; a ratio of one Representative for every 647,000 would have been irrational. (The founders proposed only three ratios; they are also in The Bill of Rights' *Article the first*: 30,000, 40,000 and 50,000.) They settled on the ratio of one for every 30,000 at the request of George Washington. Ignoring this aspect of our polity (our constitutional representation ratio) is *fracturing* America, when, in fact, the ratio was designed to *facture* (build) us.

Some may be thinking: "One for every 30,000 is too many." It wasn't to the founders; they would call one for 647,000 *usurpation*. Disregard for constitutional theory (Madison's theory) fosters confusion and destroys legitimacy. The factions (the noise) of 30,000 from the general population were/are supposed to be heard/represented in the House of Representatives. The House was designed with factions in mind; it was where we were to learn about each other, up close and personal, in a relatively unmediated way.

Not following the exact ratio isn't the point: it is the power principle that matters. We invented constitutions so we wouldn't have to keep arguing and debating these things. Unless there is something the framers and ratifiers missed about humans and power, maybe what they feared is what has happened? Hmm . . . at the least we shouldn't ignore and break the Constitution – that's kind of like disrespecting yourself, isn't it? Americans talk a lot of flag and country, of patriotism, and that is wonderful, but it is our Constitution that sets us apart from other forms of government, and one's constitution matters.

See how something takes on a life of its own – how Illinois grows into a state or how a ratio gets out of line – and it matters less how we got here and more what it Is. "What" is the key – as in, *"What is your/our Is?"*

5

As you might imagine, those who wrote, signed, and ratified the Constitution argued. They argued and debated the whole concept of a federal government for four months in Philadelphia. There was a lot of *For* and *Against*. Those in support of a federal constitution were called the Federalists; those with doubts were called the Anti-Federalists. They weren't so much against each other as they were against some of the rules and ideas being codified – things like the ratio of representation, factionalism itself, checks on power, and whether there was a need for a Bill of Rights. Through a process of debate and compromise, their work took effect in 1789. Today, we seem to believe we can curb factionalism by imposing silence, which isn't how things were designed.

Reforming the House in the spirit of the Constitution will change nearly all aspects of our political system. *"Why"* it hasn't been defended and reformed isn't the focus of this chapter. The power of incumbency is clear and well known, and that explains the most of it: also, a lack of knowledge on our part. Our focus will be on reform, on the future and not the past. *The people's key to the House is the Constitution*. We have the key and the Constitution (law), yet our House is in poor order. *We need a new House.* If we wait for the oligarchs to build our House, we'll be waiting a long time. It is something we've let slip away decade after decade, with the ratio always increasing in favor of the few. We'll talk about the few in a bit, but for now let us call it the power of incumbency. We are told how divided America is, but then something like 99 percent of Representatives are reelected. *The problem is not the elections: it's the size of the districts.* What we have and what the Constitution says are two different things – way different really.

This began to slip into an unconstitutional spirit over 200 years ago, but it's fixable every ten years, and 2010 (or 2020) is our next best time. In the United States we have worked under two rules of government: first with the Articles of Confederation, which we thought to be too weak; second, the Constitution, which appears powerless and yet all-powerful. A constitution is simply a set of agreed upon rules. One of the quirks of ours is that if you are born under one, as we are here, then the rules are just part of being a US citizen. In fact, Americans born here are born into the system. It is the naturalized citizens who get to take an oath and accept the rules. It's not like those of us born here get to vote on accepting the Constitution or not; maybe we should, part of a citizenship course in high schools – something more than just passing a test your Junior year.

There are lots of numbers in the Constitution, and since they are clear and measurable, it is easy to see their impact. Take the age limit to be president, 35. We wouldn't let a 25-year-old run for office because he or she wouldn't meet the requirement – as the number means something.

With a population of 300 million, the US House of Representatives should have more than 10,000 members and not *435*. The number *435* is not in the Constitution so don't bother looking. It is a limit set in practice in 1913 and by statute in 1929. The 70th Congress passed a usurpation law regarding itself, *2 U.S.C. 2a & 2b, Election of Senators and Representatives,* the congressional law setting the limit at *435* House members.

6

Let's look at two states, Delaware, the first to ratify the Constitution, and Illinois, the 21st, to see how representation forms a state's history. Along with the historical data on *Representation (Rep)*, I've added a column on what each state should have had for representation – the column marked *Constitutional Representation (CRep)*.

Delaware has had only one Representative to the House for practically all of its history (the only exception is two for 1810-1819). Its population has grown from 59,096 in 1790 to 783,600 in 2000. With a population of almost 800,000 and only one Representative, Delaware provides a stark example of ratio abuse; under *Constitutional Representation* Delaware would have a total of 27 Representatives and an increase in representation every ten years since 1930.

Delaware US House Representation, 1789-2010			
Year	Population	*Rep*	*CRep*
1787	estimated	1	1
1790	59,096	1	2
1800	64,273	1	3
1810	72,674	2	3
1820	72,749	1	3
1830	76,748	1	3
1840	78,085	1	3
1850	91,532	1	4
1860	112,216	1	4
1870	125,015	1	5
1880	146,608	1	5
1890	168,493	1	6
1900	184,735	1	7
1910	202,322	1	7
1920	223,003	1	8
1930	230,380	1	8
1940	266,505	1	9
1950	318,085	1	11
1960	446,292	1	15
1970	548,104	1	19
1980	594,338	1	20
1990	666,168	1	23
2000	783,600	1	27
2010	?	?	?

With Illinois we find growth in population does bring more representation – at least for a while. After becoming a state in 1818, Illinois voted to ban slavery in 1823, so there was not any "three fifths of all other Persons" issue in counting inhabitants; the aborigine were removed by war in 1832, and Illinois has no reservations.

Illinois, with 12.5 million citizens, presently has 19 Representatives in the House; this is the same number it had in 1870 when the population was only 2.5 million. The highest number of federal Representatives (27) peaked from 1910-1930. Beginning in 1940, the number of Representatives has declined from 27 to the current 19; meanwhile, population has increased from eight million to over twelve million. Under *Constitutional Representation* the number of Representatives should have increased every ten years; the only exception being 1990 when it would have remained at 381.

Illinois US House Representation, 1818-2010			
Year	Population	Rep	CRep
1818	12,282	1	1
1820	55,211	1	2
1830	157,445	3	6
1840	476,183	7	16
1850	851,470	9	29
1860	1,711,951	14	58
1870	2,539,891	19	85
1880	3,077,871	20	103
1890	3,826,352	22	128
1900	4,821,550	25	161
1910	5,638,591	27	188
1920	6,485,280	27	217
1930	7,630,654	27	255
1940	7,897,241	26	264
1950	8,712,176	25	291
1960	10,081,158	24	337
1970	11,110,285	24	371
1980	11,427,409	22	381
1990	11,430,602	20	381
2000	12,419,293	19	414
2010	13,000,000 est.	?	?

7

Our nation has changed since 1920 – though the number of Representatives hasn't; it hasn't been updated to represent women, who received the right to vote by constitutional amendment in 1920. This means women are not represented in the House according to their numbers. In fact, we have given many groups the right to vote (Civil Rights Act of 1964) over the last 85 years, but we haven't given them representation. This will not last; sooner or later the issue of representation will be politicized – *it already is when you think about it.*

Some of our fellow citizens will not like this return to constitutional augmentation of representation. The few (the oligarchy) won't. They'll want to keep the power they have and will be inclined to not share. They have a problem though; it's found in Article 6, Paragraph 3 of our Constitution: *"The Senators and Representatives before mentioned, and the Members of the several State Legislatures, and all executive and judicial Officers, both of the United States and of the several States, shall be bound by Oath or Affirmation, to support this Constitution; but no religious Test shall ever be required as a Qualification to any Office or public Trust under the United States."*

Hmm . . . this is power that can produce change; for starters, it would make the House look like us.

8

Recall the Federalists supported ratification. Three of them, Alexander Hamilton, James Madison, and John Jay, wrote a collection of essays called *The Federalist Papers*. At the time of ratification, the Federalists defended the concept of *constitutional representation*. They wrote essays to the people of New York to convince them to ratify the Constitution (which New York did). The documents make clear, and we will go into some detail below, that the Federalists believed one Representative for every 30,000 inhabitants would make the House safe, and also more importantly, *keep it safe*, in its role of balancing power.

The Convention designed the House to be a dynamic institution, bound to change, with an equal place in power. It was built to channel factionalism *into* representative government.

As the country grew in population, the ratifiers knew the number of Representatives would also grow. Writing in Federalist 55, Madison projected: *"At the expiration of twenty-five years, according to the computed rate of increase, the number of representatives will amount to two hundred, and of fifty years, to four hundred."*

The Convention agreed that the Legislative Branch would represent the people and the states. This was one of the early key compromises – called the Connecticut Compromise. They agreed to divide the legislature into two sections to split the law-making power. State representation was set at two members for all, thus making large and small states equal. The House of Representatives is where size mattered: as a state's population grew, so would representation. For example, Delaware and New York would be represented equally in the Senate with two members, and the difference in population would be represented in the House.

If we look at Article 1, Section 2, Clause 3, we can find what was agreed to and ratified. This section included the most recognizable failure of the Constitution: the *"three fifths"* deal. At the Convention, Southern states wanted slaves to count toward representation; Northern states didn't. The "compromise" was to count: *"the whole Number of free Persons, including those bound to Service for a Term of Years, and excluding Indians not taxed, three fifths of all other Persons [slaves]."* This aspect of Clause 3 was replaced by the 14th Amendment (1868).

Clause 3 also states that a census must be taken within three years of ratification – and it was – and that every ten years a census be taken for the purpose of representation – and it has been. Clause 3 also apportioned the first House based on agreement. Since there wasn't a census to work with, they simply agreed to the number of Representatives for each state. These numbers were based on a state's estimated population; for example, it was proposed that New York would begin with six Representatives and Delaware with one.

In the Senate the founders agreed to two Senators for each state; for the House they chose this wording: *"The Number of Representatives shall not exceed one for every thirty*

Thousand, but each State shall have at Least one Representative." At the time, this theory of representation – that one could represent 30,000 – it was a big deal. In the state legislatures of the period, the representation ratio was often much lower. For example, we read in Federalist 55, that in Pennsylvania the ratio was one for every four or five thousand, in Rhode Island one for a thousand, and in several Georgia districts they had an incredibly low ratio of one for ten.

People at the time realized, and we should also, that there is no magic number when it comes to ratios and representation. Madison knew this and said so in Federalist 55: *"Nothing can be more fallacious than to found our political calculations on arithmetical principles."* One for every 30,000 isn't a magical ratio that solves all of our problems and makes everyone happy. In fact, Madison warns us of thinking that a large assembly will make us a better nation. His fear of the mob was evident: *"In all very numerous assemblies, of whatever character composed, passion never fails to wrest the sceptre from reason. Had every Athenian citizen been a Socrates, every Athenian assembly would still have been a mob."*

George Washington is our Socrates. He presided over the drafting of our Constitution as *President of the Convention* and chose not to speak during the deliberations. He was silent (during debates) until the last day, 17 September 1787. After the proposed Constitution had been read aloud, he rose and announced a request. He asked those gathered to make one change: he asked them to *lower* the ratio for representation from, *"one for every forty Thousand,"* to *"one for every thirty Thousand."* The request was unanimously approved and the change was made – then they signed it.

Remember that moment: George Washington, war hero, deliverer and arguably the person most responsible for our revolution, he requested a *lowering* of the ratio to provide the House with *more* power. Yet every time since then, the Representatives have declined to keep the ratio lower: it's in their interest, and not ours, to keep representation small. Twenty-one censuses in a row and you'd think just once we'd side with Washington's leadership on *We the People's* House.

9

In Federalist 56, Madison defends the House against the charge that it: *"will be too small to possess a due knowledge of the interests of its constituents."* The founders wanted to insure local interests were represented; Madison's theories require Representatives to bring local knowledge to the federal House. The founders also believed: *"every Representative will have much information to acquire concerning all other States."*

The House wasn't (just) designed as a place to make laws: it was designed as a place of knowledge as well. Not only would a large House send more Representatives to Washington, it would also send more Representatives back home with new knowledge. The initial House had 65 members: the current has *435*. It's hard to see how *435* can come home and let 300 million of us know what's going on – thus the form letters.

10

In Federalist 57, the charge is found in the title of the essay: *The Alleged Tendency of the New Plan to Elevate the Few at the Expense of the Many Considered in Connection with*

Representation. This one paints a portrait of a House of Representatives from the general population. Madison asks: *"Who are to be the electors of the federal representatives?"* We the People is the easy answer, but he wrote it supremely:

> *Not the rich, more than the poor; not the learned, more than the ignorant; not the haughty heirs of distinguished names, more than the humble sons of obscurity and unpropitious fortune. The electors are to be the great body of the people of the United States.*

As there would be no qualification for office (*"not of wealth, of birth, of religious faith, or of civil profession"*), the people would choose a local to "confer the representative trust." In the voice of someone who believed in conferring the representative trust, Madison anticipated the relationship between the Representative and constituent to be based on: *"Duty, gratitude, interest, and ambition itself."*

Again from Federalist 57:

> *The city of Philadelphia is supposed to contain between fifty and sixty thousand souls. It will therefore form nearly two districts for the choice of federal representatives.*

Today, with an approximate population of *sixty thousand souls*, Dubuque, Iowa would be equal to the founders' Philadelphia. Today with 1.5 million souls, Philadelphia would warrant more than fifty federal Representatives under *Constitutional Representation.*

11

The previous charge might raise some eyebrows as it looks a lot like what has happened. We can look at why Madison said this wouldn't happen, as discussed in Federalist 58, and maybe we can see why one for every *thirty Thousand* is a fair and agreed upon number.

In Federalist 58, Madison again places the charge to be defended in the title: *"Objection That The Number of Members Will Not Be Augmented as the Progress of Population Demands Considered."* Madison and the others saw the problem clearly and even anticipated what we now face. Here is also where we see an assumption made by the Constitutional Convention breakdown: *the founders thought the large states would defend this principle.*

Perhaps it just hasn't happened yet, as it probably will be the large states that will demand House augmentation. Madison: *"There is a peculiarity in the federal Constitution which insures a watchful attention in a majority both of the people and of their representatives to a constitutional augmentation of the latter."*

I see how Madison is still going to be correct; he and the others thought augmentation would take place because the general population in the larger states would demand it. If states like California, New York, Texas, Florida, Illinois, Michigan, and Ohio, if they demanded constitutional representation, they would achieve it.

This "peculiarity" hasn't materialized only because the large states haven't demanded it. Madison wrote that from the interest of the large states: *"it may with certainty be inferred that the larger States will be strenuous advocates for increasing the number and weight of that part of the legislature in which their influence predominates."* Madison argued that if there were problems, the general population could step in by building a coalition of the constitutionally willing:

> *Should the representatives or people, therefore, of the smaller States oppose at any time a reasonable addition of members, a coalition of a very few States will be sufficient to overrule the opposition; a coalition which, notwithstanding the rivalship and local prejudices which might prevent it on ordinary occasions, would not fail to take place, when not merely prompted by common interest, but justified by equity and the principles of the Constitution.*

12

The peculiarity that Madison talked about is hibernating. One can fault the people for not knowing, but the Representatives know: they take the oath.

We've lost touch with a government we've lost interest in. What we have now is oligarchy and it's going to keep causing problems: like going to war and never declaring it and/or waiting for peace and never making it.

We will hear all kinds of things in our new House of representation; in fact, we'll have to build a *new* US House of Representatives in order to have enough seats for everyone. A reading of *The Federalist Papers* shows the House was designed to be noisy. We have become a nation of *public opinion polls* rather than *public opinion makers*. The general population has surrendered its *voices* without knowing it; instead of moving into a bigger House to accommodate our growing population (more factions), Congress moved to keep factions out – contrary to our founding's constitutional logic.

One Representative for every *thirty Thousand* makes everything closer, bridging distance in ways editorials and episodes of The Simpsons cannot.

13

The Representatives themselves, how different they would look if their districts were 21 times smaller than they are today. There would still be your media stars and party positions, though even that influence would be different.

One for every *thirty Thousand* would challenge the two party system and they would adapt. It would allow for open, unaffiliated candidates. I grew up in Illinois' Jo Daviess County, which borders Iowa and Wisconsin; the county's population is about 28,000, so basically, due to Illinois' geography/borders, someone local would be going to Washington. *(That sounds good to me.)* The interests, concerns and ideas of Jo Daviess County would be represented in Congress. *(That sounds even better to me.)*

Media would be deepened and dispersed. With 10,000 Representatives for a population of 300 million, there would be more to cover and more to understand. With many

Representatives, they would reflect their communities. There would actually be different kinds of people – Arab-Americans, for example – in the House, so we would have some human intelligence on cultures and religions. You might see your Representative getting his or her coffee in the morning, or not going to church on Sunday, or taking in a local Blue Grass festival. You might have the occasion to see your Representative at the grocery store buying red potatoes and an inexpensive Merlot. Citizens would have a much easier time getting to know a federal Representative, and *vice versa*.

Corporations and individuals would still try to control the process with money, though the money would be dispersed based on population and not consolidated by incumbency.

A new House would move factionalism about issues like racism, classism and religion, it would take that factionalism and move it to a political realm where it can be discussed, debated, and resolved. (Yes, resolved.) For example, and almost by definition, the more you know about someone the less likely you are to be ignorant. As Madison noted in Federalist 55, our Representatives were to take knowledge home – back to our communities. They were to speak *as and for* American citizens. Perhaps they would report things like "Arab-Americans aren't . . . " and perhaps they would speak of things the television won't touch because it doesn't sell advertising.

14

Let's examine Congress' war-making power (Article 1, Section 8) and discuss how a constitutional House would change things. Politics is driven by both rationality and irrationality. As we gather in a House of thousands instead of hundreds we will see different results. *We the People* talking is constitutionalism, the antidote to anarchy *and* oligarchy.

In 2003, syndicated columnist David Broder wrote about Congress and its lack of support for war responsibilities. I agree with him, as today Representatives can vote for war resolutions without suffering any possible election disadvantage – they can put the responsibility and blame on the commander-in-chief and our generals. Look at the election in 2004, not between President Bush and Senator Kerry, but at how divided we were over war and yet practically every federal Representative gets reelected – every time, every election. Half of this argument appears in Broder's essay, aptly titled: "Congress shrinks from war responsibilities – members ignoring the Constitution." Broder referred to the lack of a war declaration as an institutional failure: more to our point, it is a constitutional failure. Broder provides a wordy quote from our House of Representatives International Relations Committee Report – rather than a constitutional declaration of war – supporting the invasion of Iraq. This is where the language about presidential use of force comes up; we are told, constitutionally speaking, this means war, except there is no declaration of war, constitutionally. Here's how the House committee put it:

> The committee hopes that the use of military force can be avoided. It believes, however, that providing the president with the authority he needs to use force is the best way to avoid its use.

So we are going to provide the commander-in-chief, any of them, as this will happen again, we are going to provide them the authority to use force as the best way to avoid its use. Hmm. That's like saying: *"I'm going to give you this weapon (power) as the best way to avoid its use."* I don't think that sort of logic works well in war. If chosen or forced upon, almost everyone agrees war should be done with clear intentions. See how the House fails us in this role? The House, in its small size and large ratio, it doesn't inform the government how the general population feels. Opinion polls aren't the same as debate. Too often President Bush is taking the heat for the Iraq operation, but it is the House that is failing us institutionally; Bush is using the power available and that is his option. All this *"use of military force"* isn't a declaration of war though: Article 1, Section 8 of our Constitution says Congress shall, *"declare War."*

Broder closes his essay with a traditional call for Congress to "reassert its role." It isn't Congress who is shirking their responsibilities, but us, the citizens. If there isn't constitutional representation, then they aren't following the most basic of rules, and there appears to be no way of controlling them, unless they affirm the words they swore to uphold; until that happens, they aren't representing the general population or the Constitution, in war or any other topic.

Recall the days after September 11th as we saw it all begin. On Friday, 14 September, the House of Representatives approved a resolution authorizing President Bush to "use all necessary and appropriate force" against the perpetrators of the deadly terrorist attack. The Senate passes the measure the same day. Saturday, 15 September, President Bush says the United States is *"at war."* Tuesday, 18 September, Bush signs the Congressional resolution authorizing military action against those behind the attacks. That's been over three years now . . . *what does the end look like?*

15

Members of Congress sang on the steps of the Capitol; it was the evening of September 11th, and they were there for a news conference. Before the news conference they sang *God Bless America* and not our national anthem, *The Star-Spangled Banner.* Singing the anthem, a song about bravery under attack during the Battle of Baltimore (17 September 1814), that would have been appropriate – particularly given the fact that Muslims, Christians and Jews pray to the same God, *the God of Abraham.* Nonetheless, I was saddened to see so few, knowing how many could have been there – the thousands instead of the hundreds – knowing there could be, constitutionally, over 10,000 singers, a chorus of 10,000 Representatives and 100 Senators, and them singing a song – whichever song – that would have been impressive. It would have been Americans of all types singing together and reflecting a unified country in a way *435 plus 100 just can't do.*

The general theory of power in our Constitution is dispersion; separate power to keep any one group or faction from consolidating it. Conversely, through dispersion, power of a kind increases: the power of *We the People.* In our citizens – that's our collective genius. The Senate was designed to represent the states: the House was designed to represent the inhabitants of each state. By trading representation for a small House, power has not been dispersed, but consolidated.

16

The question is clear: *how is it that we don't accept George Washington's law as it is written in our Constitution?*

Most Americans would tell you that *constitutional law beats congressional law.* For example, we wouldn't let a Congress pass a law changing the requirement concerning the age of a Representative or presidential citizenship; you'd have to amend the Constitution in order to bring about that sort of change.

It appears that in order to get our representative power back, all we have to do is ask. As humans, we often bemoan our situation instead of looking around at what is available. The Constitution is available to us and loaded with under-utilized power. That power is located, not in the number of Representatives *per se*, but in the power of sharing and communicating local information. A House in which there are only 435 representing 300 million does not provide this function today. According to the design of our Constitution, the strength and genius of the American people is in our power to channel factionalism. We have been known to exclude whole groups – "Indians not taxed" – and made the worth of others a percent of an ideal – "three fifths of all other Persons." The Is takes the Constitution as is: a code of self-government. Unlike religious texts, the Constitution was ratified; that means it was accepted by *We the People* and not by a single act of a Congress.

One thing is for sure: nothing will happen unless the general population begins talking about this; they, the few, will offer compromises and diversions, but staying the constitutional course will make them build a House of Representatives for the many. As mentioned above, they have to if words still mean anything.

Here's *The Oath* again; it merits a second reading: *"The Senators and Representatives before mentioned, and the Members of the several State Legislatures, and all executive and judicial Officers, both of the United States and of the several States, shall be bound by Oath or Affirmation, to support this Constitution; but no religious Test shall ever be required as a Qualification to any Office or public Trust under the United States."*

Those are clear words, self-evident you might say, and individuals like George Washington saw fit to risk it all for them. Remind yourself of him standing there on the last day of the Convention; imagine him mulling over the idea of lowering the ratio of Representative to represented. He had a thought come to mind; he made a decision on the merits of the matter, in his brain, with him thinking something in the affirmative like, *"Yes, this is a good thing."* He then mentions the change, the change to a smaller ratio and larger House, and a vote is taken: unanimous.

Washington recommended lowering the ratio from the agreed upon one for every *forty Thousand* to the still constitutional ratio of one for every *thirty Thousand*. Washington sat there all summer and didn't say a thing – not a thing – during all of the debates, not until the end, and then he spoke to us – perhaps even to us in the future – and he asked that the ratio be lowered, which means he wanted a large House. When this change arrives, as it will, sooner or later, it will be interesting to see if Washington's ideas and intentions are heard; like Derrida said of Nietzsche – it is the *ear of the other* that marks one's signature, as it is the present that has the power to uphold George Washington's wish, not him or the past. So recall the circle and imagine, if you will, in part of the circle are the current incumbents, the few, representing the current state of the Constitution, and in another part are Madison, Hamilton, Jay, Franklin, and Washington, representing the words and spirit of the Constitution: the question remaining – *Where are you?*

William Pierce, an attendee at the Convention, would be with Washington. During the summer Pierce wrote brief sketches about the men in attendance. About George Washington he noted: *"Having conducted these states to independence and peace, he now appears to assist in framing a Government to make the People happy. Like Gustavus Vasa, he may be said to be the deliverer of his Country."*

Yes, but as we've seen, it isn't always so easy to follow the advice of a deliverer.

4

Epimorphosis
(Or, Where's that confounded bridge?)

1

Jazzercise – what if every day started with jazzercise?

Every decision you make, every thought you have, is a chemical reaction of neurotransmitters and electrical impulses. When you feel love or hate, sickness or health, and any other dialectic or order of thought, it, all of it, remains a combination of chemicals and electrical impulses. Such knowledge has yet to have any discernible impact on our politics, and there is no certainty that it will; possibly though, it takes something ephemeral and makes it more understood. If my sense-of-myself is chemical and electrical, then this is also how my body is, and how it all Is.

Being and body have long been divisible. That is no longer a necessity – if it ever was. Divisible and indivisible are ideals, and, like all things, can be judged (deemed and valued) as good, but the good can always be other, which could be not good. In a sense, all human values can be turned on their head: they can be inverted. Abraham, Sun Tzu, Jesus, Hegel, Marx, Nietzsche, Freud, and the list goes on and on. History itself is this list of values and their overturning.

In his essay "The Metaphysics of the Code," Jean Baudrillard opens with a discussion of the binary system, the 0 and 1 world of Liebniz and other utopians. Utopians are thinkers that privilege the implementation of an ideal. Baudrillard is a well-known "post-modern" thinker. He specializes in something like the *reductio ad absurdum* (reduction to absurdity): *one must accept the thesis because rejection is untenable*. For instance, in thinking, if you endlessly reduce you eventually end up with nothing. It's a point of zero-ness that is in the realm of human emotions. You see, to deny nothingness becomes difficult because humans say they feel it. Yet isn't that the question we face:

what is human feeling? If it is talked of as chemical and electrical impulse, as science tells us it is, then does that change how we think? For instance, if you read of some new research in the magazine *Scientific American*, how does it affect your thinking?

Reductio ad absurdum is a way of thinking. Baudrillard isn't an advocate for this way of thinking (not necessarily), he's just pointing out that many of our basic assumptions have become necessities and that refuting them is unthinkable. The world stops making sense to people at a point (including me). We might think, *"Big deal, right?"* I have found that if you talk to people about this, two things usually pop up: romanticism or fatalism. There is either a happy ending or the hope that it isn't too bad of an ending. The only real difference between the two is that the romantic shows more feeling than the fatalist.

Baudrillard also points out that transitions in the code also create other transitions. He notes that *the biological theorization of the code* (such as DNA explaining the meaning of life) prepares the way for a new order that aims at total control. There's some truth in there – the part about the code and controlling people. The body is first and foremost a *sensorium* (the sum of an organism's perception). It is changeable in ways the soul and ego are not: the soul and ego can hide, but sense has *less* ability to do so. Concepts like the soul and ego code the messages of the senses. Even consciousness gets some time off once in a while, through leisure or sleep for instance, but the body is full time work even when resting. It doesn't stop until the end.

Today, DNA itself has undergone a trans-valuation (a change). It seems that much of what was referred to as *"junk"* DNA is actually becoming *valued* DNA. No surprises there really, as the code is resilient. The part of the code that is now being studied, the previously junk DNA, will no doubt be more convincing than DNA could ever have been. That is how science works: clarity and doubt combined, and in it Baudrillard's point is maintained. Issues of transcendence die: whom they die for is a political matter. I may believe God is dead – meaning the theory of monotheism is not convincing to me – but that is only part of my Is and of the Is I live (my sensorium).

I also believe progress is dead – meaning the theory that progress is other than a human cost-benefit reduction. If you have a high standard of doubt, then progress is a measure of irreconcilable values; progress, as an idea and practice, is culturally specific. Look at what was good for the aborigine leader Black Hawk and what was good for the progress of the state of Illinois, and see how they were in conflict. The good of one meant the death of the other, and *vice versa*. Put simply, progress (p) is always greater than 1 [p > 1]. It involves more than one idea, more than one perspective, more than one-way. Progress itself is contestatory, just like war.

2

Epimorphosis is just a fancy name for new growth. The prefix *"epi"* has many meanings of time and place, indicating a relation – a preposition – such as on/upon/over/above/near/beside and after. The prefix also refers to: *"a chemical substance related to a specified chemical substance."* The center part of the word, *"morpho,"* means to shape or form. The suffix *"sis"* is used to show process and action. All three parts come from the

Greek language. Separately, they mean *on/upon*, *shape/form*, and *process/action*. Together: *"the regeneration of a part of an organ characterized by proliferation of new tissue."*

Epimorphosis is akin to thinking. We have to recall memories and ideas and our accumulated knowledge. When we recall something, we have to regenerate the synapses. This brings whatever it is we are thinking about into being (to life). It wasn't dead either, just not active. Epimorphosis bridges, and in thinking, it is a chemical bridge. Through our action and inaction (Is), we make the world around us. To make the unknown familiar, we use seduction: something to keep and hold interest. By virtue of a busy world, with the programming of information and the standardness of education, we tend toward the unimaginative (it's all been done); this creates a world where the possible seems rote and the impossible redundant.

We see an unimaginative way of thinking, or perhaps an over-imaginative way, when we look at America's history of segregation. Segregation was enforced by a set of laws referred to as *"Jim Crow."* These laws enforced the public display of internal intolerance. For example, at this time throughout the South, white and black Americans did not drink out of the same public water fountains. Bigot or not, some people would have thought of ending segregation and what it would mean to drink from the same fountain as . . . well you can see how that thought, that thought of not knowing who drank from that fountain, well you can see how fear of the unknown worked to keep people segregated. Fear works well in the realm of the unknown, and the fear of unknown lips may have kept many on the sidelines. Humans don't need much of an excuse to stand aside or to stand up – we're unique that way.

3

There's a story told about editing that involves the Declaration of Independence. It seems Thomas Jefferson, the main writer of the document, at first had written: *"We hold these truths to be sacred and undeniable."* To show you the subtle power of words, Ben Franklin, a rationalist as opposed to the religious Jefferson, substituted the words we are more familiar with: *"We hold these truths to be self-evident."*

The *right to consciousness* is a brewing battle in the United States. What started as freedom of religion is morphing into freedom of consciousness. We find the battle being played out in the world of public safety and personal responsibility, and perhaps the most common battlefield is the drug war and the judicial system.

The idea that humans are unable to use cannabis responsibly is a myth. Cannabis is a plant and humans have been using it for eons. Writers write to make sense of something. If you write about alcohol and how it enters the body through the stomach, liver and blood, and how it gets into your system and makes you, at some point, if you drink enough of it, intoxicated, then you are writing about the body and feelings. The feeling of intoxication has highs and lows and ups and downs. Some people abuse alcohol, but most don't have a problem with it. We regulate the alcohol industry and tax those who produce and consume it. We tried prohibiting alcohol, and did so through an Amendment, but that didn't work; it created more problems, like violence, and not enough taxes – and people were still drinking. The *possession* of alcohol wasn't illegal, just *"the manufacture, sale, or transportation of intoxicating liquors."* Cannabis prohibition is one step more intrusive: *possession* is a federal crime.

Cannabis, known to many as marijuana, also can enter the body through the stomach, liver and blood. It can also be inhaled, either through smoking or vaporizing. In both cases, initially and briefly, the cannabinoids enter the blood and do nothing. A cannabinoid is inactive in the body until it connects with a *cannabinoid receptor* – no receptors and no reaction.

I first read about this difference from alcohol in 2001 in a book called *The Science of Marijuana*. The author, Leslie Iverson, wrote that all humans have a cannabinoid system and "naturally occurring chemicals" known as *endocannabinoids*. He even noted that this field of research had changed: *"from a pharmacological study of how the psychoactive drug THC works in the brain to a much broader field of biological research on a unique natural control system."* Cannabinoids modulate the entire body – not just the brain. That means, foremost, that it's not about "getting high," that biologically the health effects are more interesting than the psychoactive ones – or that the two go together in ways we typically don't imagine.

This demystifies the cannabis high; humans have a cannabinoid system that produces endocannabinoids: *"endo-"* means inside and *"cannabinoid"* comes from the plant's science name, *Cannabis sativa*. This system has a biologic effect designed by God, evolution or any other model. Every human being has had cannabinoid receptors: Abraham, Socrates, Jesus, Washington, etc. I'll discuss these receptors and the reactions they produce below, but for now think of them as places in the body where cannabinoids connect. These receptors are located throughout us – literally, from head to toe.

Let's look at three summary statements before proceeding:

- Humans have a cannabinoid system
- Humans make cannabinoids
- Humans consume cannabinoids

Next, we're going to "de-moralize" cannabis for a moment (a chapter) and take a biological look; we can always "re-moralize" it later if needed.

4

Science and cannabis politics brought us to this point. I think cannabis should be regulated and taxed. Cannabis use isn't a criminal act. In fact, more people should use cannabis. I'm not arguing that cannabis isn't as bad as alcohol; I'm arguing that science says cannabis is good. The word should be discussed in terms of "health care" and not "drug war." Cannabis can be abused, but so can anything; religion and television come to mind. More importantly, cannabis can be of use, like religion and television.

It wasn't until 1964 that Raphael Mechoulam of the Hebrew University in Jerusalem identified the most active psychological agent in cannabis. Most of us have heard it called THC: the science name is *delta-9-tetrahydrocannabinol*. This plant cannabinoid is the most well known, but there are many more. Another plant cannabinoid named earlier, in 1942 at the University of Illinois by Roger Adams, is called Cannabidiol (CBD). There are also many pharmaceutical (synthetic) cannabinoids.

Scientific American noted in 2004 that cannabinoid receptors are: *"small proteins embedded in the membranes of all cells, including neurons."* When cannabinoids bind with these receptors a change occurs. Some receptors allow electricity (chemical ions) to pass in or out of the cell. Others specialize in proteins. The so-called "G-proteins" are quite plentiful and set in motion a whole series of biochemical signaling. For instance, these protein receptors are found in abundance in the brain and central nervous system, to include the hypothalamus, basal ganglia, cerebral cortex, hippocampus, cerebellum, brain stem, spinal cord and amygdala.

The first cannabinoid receptors weren't located until 1988. Receptors were found by attaching radioactive tags to synthetic THC molecules; they then followed them to see where they attached. The first receptor they found they named "CB1." Once they knew what they were looking for they began to find the receptors all over the brain, with high densities throughout numerous regions. Since then, another receptor, one named "CB2," has been identified; its principle function appears to be the immune system. The pervasiveness of these receptors throughout the body accounts for the omnipresent effects of cannabinoids.

5

A right to consciousness is a right to body: it's called liberty and freedom (they go together). Some don't want the freedom; they want to make the body pay for something else: sin, redemption or a psychological observation.

There is a will to health in humans and it is found in how we adapt to our environment. Standing upright was part of this process; the ability to run was another big development. Running let us travel farther, which increased our perspective and information; more information led to more of almost everything else.

"Running made us human, at least in an anatomical sense," stated a researcher in a 2004 *Nature* article in the New York Times. About two million years ago humans began to develop different bodies: our legs got longer, buttocks stronger, pelvis narrowed and arms shortened. Science also says that a ligament grew into place at the base of our skull to hold our head steady while running (otherwise I guess it would have flopped around). Utilizing the physical evidence, we can trace out this beginning. The Old Testament doesn't explain things like this; in that narrative it seems we were just made to run.

6

Cannabis consumption is as natural to the body as running, and cannabinoid receptors have been around longer than running – a lot longer – about 498 million years longer. That's according to "The Brain's Own Marijuana," a 2004 *Scientific American* article:

> *The receptor CB1 seems to be present in all vertebrate species, suggesting that systems employing the brain's own marijuana have been in existence for about 500 million years.*

The article isn't kidding; it continues on with the following:

> *During that time, endocannabinoids have been adapted to serve numerous, often subtle, functions. We have learned that they do not affect the development of fear, but the forgetting of fear; they do not alter the ability to eat, but the desirability of the food, and so on. Their presence in parts of the brain associated with complex motor behavior, cognition, learning and memory implies that much remains to be discovered about the uses to which evolution has put these interesting messengers.*

Yes they are, those cannabinoids – *interesting messengers*. That's a good way to put it.

To understand how messages are delivered, to see how cannabinoids work in a physical activity, here's another bit of new research that paints an interesting picture of the body in exercise. The article, "Exercise activates the endocannabinoid system," was published in December 2003 in the *NeuroReport – Cognitive Neuroscience and Neuropsychology*.

The *runner's high* is produced by the cannabinoid system during and after physical activities (things that make you sweat). For a long time it was thought endorphins explained this chemical aspect of what runner's report; endorphins cannot readily cross the "blood-brain barrier" though. This barrier is a filter built into our bodies that doesn't allow certain chemicals to pass into the brain. This filter is also one of the main barriers to the delivery of pharmaceuticals inside the brain.

We know that exercise has analgesic (*we feel better*) and sedative (*we relax*) effects. What the new research shows is that the runner's high is attributable to an increase in the production of *anandamide*, the first endocannabinoid identified by science.

One can also note running raised anandamide levels in early humans – the first runner's high. Endocannabinoids have been around for 500 million years in all vertebrate animals. In other words, given the biology of thinking, one can say that *endocannabinoids made us human, at least in the genetic sense.*

7

The *NeuroReport* article, written by researchers from the Georgia Institute of Technology, University of California (Irvine), and Georgia College and State University, shows that after running or cycling for 50 minutes, all 24 male participants had statistically elevated levels of anandamide. They noted that only anandamide levels were statistically significant for their testing; the levels of another endocannabinoid, 2-AG, were also elevated, but they concluded that 2-AG: *"is synthesized via different biochemical pathways and may be produced under different conditions."* Their hypothesis (via different biochemical pathways) will be discussed below; for now, notice how *dependent* thinking is on cannabinoids; it would be false to hypothesize the opposite (that thinking is *independent* of cannabinoids).

The *NeuroReport* notes how we are wired for anandamide:

- It is *"synthesized in and released from a variety of peripheral cells, including sensory neurons."*
- It *"causes profound antinociceptive and antihyperalgesic effects, which are mediated by CB1 cannabinoid receptors on pain-sensing C fibers."*

Those fancy science words *antinociceptive* and *antihyperalgesic* mean a body senses and finds *relief from pain.*

Do you see why a war on cannabis consumers, those who inhale, through a vaporizer or smoke, or those who ingest, through food or a tincture, isn't going to last? When marijuana prohibition started no one knew any of this. Everyone thought getting high on marijuana was like getting drunk: it's not.

8

I've been a runner myself. Through basketball and Army conditioning I got used to it. I also found the more I ran the more I liked it. (Lots of people report the same.) Running has been part of the exercise routine for the last three US presidents. In October of 2002, President Bush did an interview on how running has helped him; Bob Wischnia and Paul Carrozza interviewed him for *Runner's World* and it is published online. The first question they asked President Bush: *"What role does running play in your mental and physical fitness?"* He said it was very important and that's why he runs five or six days a week. He went on to say running:

- helps me sleep at night
- keeps me disciplined
- breaks up my day
- allows me to recharge my batteries
- enables me to set goals and push myself toward those goals
- in essence, it keeps me young
- adds a little bounce to my step
- I get a certain amount of self-esteem from it
- I just look and feel better

His quotes are all from the first question!

In the second question he is asked about stress: *"You must have the most stressful job in the world. Does running help you cope with that level of stress?"* President Bush replied that it does help with stress; he then mentions that his running times have become faster since the war on terror began:

They were pretty fast all along, but since the war began, I have been running with a little more intensity. And I guess that's part of the stress relief I get from it. For me, the psychological benefit is enormous. You tend to forget everything that's going on in your mind and just concentrate on the time, distance or the sweat. It helps me clear my mind.

Recall that cannabinoids, both endogenous and exogenous, cross the blood-brain barrier and that anandamide accounts for the runner's high. We know what is physically happening to President Bush's body while running; with exercise, his cannabinoid levels are increasing, in particular, his level of anandamide. The psychological benefit President Bush reports, the chemical helping him to clear his mind, is the endocannabinoid anandamide; it's being produced and is activating the CB1 receptors in his brain.

9

Cannabinoids are the reason President Bush is finding enormous health benefits from running. He started running in 1972 (age 25) after getting out of the service. He said in the *Runner's World* interview that he started running because of health concerns: *"Back then, I was a man known to drink a beer or two. And over time, I'm convinced that running helped me quit drinking and smoking."*

Running produces the cannabinoid anandamide; it is activity (exercise) that increases anandamide levels. Repetitive action stimulates the production of cannabinoids; this production causes the healing effect that President Bush and others report. Later in the interview he is asked about running and how it helped him quit alcohol:

Definitely. As a runner, I quickly realized what it felt like to be healthy and I already knew what it felt like to be unhealthy. If you're drinking too much and you're running to cure a hangover, pretty soon you have to make a choice. Do you want to keep getting a hangover or do you want to feel the way you do after a run? So running is a way to heal people. Running is something that just makes you feel fantastic.

Yes, President Bush and I share a love for cannabinoids.

10

I'm glad President Bush can run and enjoy exercising his cannabinoid system; that's normal. We wouldn't think of coercing citizens to run, not in the land of the free. Listen to some of your favorite musicians and think of coercing them to be "normal."

According to a new line of synthetic (pharmaceutical) cannabinoids, a new normal may be on the horizon; it's called *Rimonobant* and it's being marketed as treatment for "marijuana dependence." The National Institute of Drug Abuse (NIDA) has even claimed one dose will cure you of marijuana dependence. Wow. Lucky for music lovers these future "treatments" weren't around any earlier. Any Jazz fans out there? Try taking cannabis out of the beginning of Jazz and you'd be taking away Jazz. I don't mean you have to be high on cannabinoids to enjoy Jazz, but a certain one-of-a-kind musician named Louis Armstrong, well he called pot his friend (his assistant) and I believe he would have agreed with President Bush; one can find "enormous psychological benefit," healing and "a clearing of the mind" by activating your cannabinoid system.

The forgetting, well, I have a theory on that too; I'll bet it let Armstrong forget a lot of the racism he had to face, or anything else we all go through. Cannabinoids don't make you forget who you are; President Bush doesn't forget who he is while running. You don't forget what is important to you or what you need to do; the highs let you pause and forget the day for a moment. Many people have experienced such highs and describe the same benefits as President Bush; they just find relief and healing from consuming a plant instead of from running.

What of those who don't have the same running ability as President Bush, or who can't run or exercise as easily, but they want the same benefits from cannabinoids? And lots of people have activated their cannabinoid system through cannabis to quit alcohol and tobacco – just like President Bush.

11

The *Scientific American* article has a diagram on *"retrograde signaling."* This four part diagram is discussed, in print and online, in six sentences that provide a clear example of a sense~chemical combination (a sensorium). Cannabinoids are the main messengers in *retrograde signaling*, a process where cells *talk back* to each other.

The six sentences show sense and chemicals working together to create the basis of action. Also, given the topic, the body's brain, one of the advantages we have is that we all have what we are discussing – a brain (so turn yours to *On*).

The first sentence from the diagram (page 88) is this:

> 1. *Researchers have found that endogenous cannabinoids (endo-cannabinoids) participate in retrograde signaling, a previously unknown form of communication in the brain.*

So science is saying cannabinoids participate in a previously unknown form of communication in the brain, retrograde signaling. The next sentence explains what that means:

> 2. *Rather than flowing forward in the usual way from a presynaptic (neurotransmitter-emitting) neuron to a postsynaptic (recipient) one, endocannabinoids work backward, traveling from the postsynaptic cell to the presynaptic one.*

Previously, science could only see cells communicating in one direction. They thought one cell emitted information and another cell received information. After the discovery of cannabinoids and their receptors, they noticed that cells were modulating their activity without receiving any information. Something in the brain was telling cells to stop firing, which then allowed other cells to fire (to be heard, so to speak). Next, using 2-AG as the example, we find that:

> 3. *The endocannabinoid 2-AG released from a postsynaptic cell can, for example, cause a presynaptic cell to decrease its secretion of the inhibitory neurotransmitter GABA onto the postsynaptic cell.*

Here we have an example of neurotransmitters in action. From a so-called receiving cell, post-synapse (meaning message conveyed), we see the creation and release of the endocannabinoid 2-AG. This cannabinoid tells the emitting cell something like, *"Hey, slow down there,"* thus decreasing the creation of another neurotransmitter called GABA. This signaling back is only the first step in retrograde signaling (there's more); it also allows other things to happen:

> 4. *If GABA from a presynaptic neuron hits a postsynaptic cell at the same time as excitatory signals (such as those carried by the neurotransmitter glutamate) reach the same cell, the GABA can block the postsynaptic cell from firing.*

Here they are saying more than one thing can happen in the brain at one time. One neurotransmitter (GABA) can block an excitatory neurotransmitter like glutamate – but then:

> 5. *If, however, changes in calcium levels in the postsynaptic neuron trigger the production of 2-AG, this endocannabinoid will travel back to its receptor (CB1) on the GABA-producing neuron.*

If there is enough 2-AG produced because of the rising calcium levels in the brain (a sign the brain is active), then the CB1 receptor activates because of the 2-AG and … :

> 6. *In a process known as depolarized-induced suppression of inhibition (DSI), it will then prevent the release of GABA and thus allow the excitatory signals to activate the postsynaptic cell.*

There's the *retrograde* kicker: the cannabinoid, in telling one cell to stop firing for a moment produces the conditions for "DSI" (allowing other signals to be sent and received). Basically, DSI tells one cell to be quiet for a moment so that another cell can talk, making it fundamental to cell communication.

That brings us back to *Rimonabant* and curing "marijuana dependence." The pharmaceutical companies are well aware of the cannabinoid system; they use synthetic cannabinoids in research and are trying to market them. *Rimonabant* is being presented to the Food and Drug Administration for US sale. Researchers at NIDA gleefully reported that a single dose of the drug blocks the effects of smoked marijuana; unfortunately, it also *blocks* endocannabinoids such as anandamide, which means it also blocks retrograde signaling (DSI), *a previously unknown form of communication in the brain.*

12

Jazzercise – that's right, I mentioned jazzercise, didn't I. You might not miss it if it disappeared, but I hear it's good exercise. Many would miss Jazz though, as it was a pretty good invention. Today, Armstrong would be labeled a marijuana addict and perhaps even put into coerced treatment. What an odd political thought: *no Jazz because all the jazzers were sent to treatment and cured.* Armstrong was a cannabis consumer, that's for sure, and he wouldn't understand today's cannabis fuss.

It's been said that Armstrong told stories with his cornet. At the 2001 tribute, *From Lincoln Center – Louis Armstrong: Master Interpreter*, Ed Bradley (of *60 Minutes* fame) said these kind words about Armstrong's Chicago music-making days:

> *On a series of records made in Chicago during the 1920s, Louis Armstrong almost single-handedly set out the foundations of Jazz. Some of the most fertile and overwhelming music in all of recorded Jazz gushes from those old discs by Louis Armstrong's Hot Five and Hot Seven Bands.*

Later on in the tribute, when they are talking about the great Joe "King" Oliver and the New Orleans roots of Jazz, Bradley tells us about how Oliver and Armstrong wowed'em in Chicago:

> *Oliver taught Armstrong about breaks – short unaccompanied solos played at the end of a musical phrase. When Armstrong played with Oliver, the sound of their two powerful horns playing breaks – in unison – amazed the crowd that packed Chicago's Lincoln Gardens. The secret? Oliver would tip Armstrong off by surreptitiously fingering what he was going to play.*

When it comes to Armstrong, his music, and his cannabis use, the show brings them together but only in a general way. Here's what Bradley said:

> *Alcohol and drugs figure into the story of many a Jazz musician but Armstrong was very health-conscious. He didn't drink heavily, but acknowledged an affection for marijuana, which he found soothing and medicinal. Armstrong and Earl Hines named one of their collaborations after one of marijuana's more closely-held nicknames, "Muggles."*

Trumpeter Nicholas Payton and pianist Eric Reed then performed the song.

13

To deny cannabinoids is to deny the body, which is a *reductio ad absurdum*. Cannabis prohibition is prohibiting us from ourselves; it weakens us by weakening our bodies (our cannabinoid systems). Ending it will be a knowledge victory.

14

In the battle for consciousness we may need a *political blood-brain barrier*; think of the future and how the next *"previously unknown form of communication"* will impact things. This time it was retrograde signaling, next time it will be . . . you see how complicated it gets. DSI is important to thinking because it allows a cell to learn and to strengthen memories. I know the myth about cannabis and cannabinoids is that it influences memory and learning in a negative way: this is not true.

Through DSI, cannabinoids allow cells to pause so they can learn other things. Sometimes in our busy body and world we need to pause; in fact, we have to forget things all the time, on purpose and by design. *Scientific American* said it this way: *"Thus, DSI, which is a short-lived local effect, enables individual neurons to disconnect briefly from their neighbors and encode information."*

Consciousness is individual (unique). We share the same chemicals but we put them together in a particular way and then call it our own. Consciousness is what is special about being human. DSI is nature's way of allowing neurons to do something other than just keep firing; it gives them time to pause in order to encode information (store memories).

In 2001 President Bush honored the influence of African-American musicians by presidential proclamation. He mentioned the long history of influence and contributions by many, and he mentioned Louis Armstrong, as well as Dizzy Gillespie, another known cannabis consumer, toward the end of his proclamation. He mentioned the word "genius" regarding their talents: *"The trumpeting genius of Louis Armstrong and Dizzy Gillespie illustrate the exceptional musicianship so prominent in various genres of African-American music."* In his remarks during the event, posted online, President Bush even mentioned Armstrong again:

> *Stories told about Louis Armstrong – someone came up to the legendary giant one day and asked him to define Jazz. They wanted to understand it, so they came to the master himself. And he replied, "Man, if you've got to ask, you'll never know." (Laughter) Well, there are some things I know today. I know America is a richer place for the musicians and the music that we honor today. Again, I welcome you to the White House. And it's now my honor to sign the executive proclamation. (Applause)*

He's correct: America is a richer place because of Dizzy Gillespie and Louis Armstrong.

15

Change comes in all forms, metaphysical and physical. If you go through an experience, it changes you. Think of tolerance: if at one time in your life you were intolerant, how did that feel to you? Did you judge harshly? Were you too demanding? – Of others or yourself?

One begins to see the chemical complexity of feelings and consciousness. Tolerance appears as understanding, compassion and joy. There's a book on the beginning of Jazz told by an original Chicago-jazzer, "Mezz" Mezzrow; his city-corner was Western and Division, now home to *Roberto Clemente High School*. In *Really the Blues*, Mezz talks about the use of cannabis in the 1920s Chicago music scene. This was before the 1937 prohibition, so cannabis wasn't even illegal yet and you could smoke it without hassle.

During one of Mezz's first highs, after smoking up in the bathroom, he took the stage to play his horn and the room came alive: *too alive*. Mezz couldn't hear his own horn playing; it unnerved him; the room was spinning and filled with noise – not music, just a thumping sound. After a few moments he realized what he was hearing: *his heart.*

Mezz had one of those notorious, startling highs and was unnerved. We all have a heart, but to hear the rhythm itself can be unnerving. If one thinks of Mezz's cannabinoid receptors, we can imagine they were popping like they'd never popped before.

We're genetically designed for cannabinoids: they're there to heal health. The more one learns about cannabinoids, the more one sees them as part of *our* nature.

16

When I see a running event like the Chicago marathon, I see a celebration of human effort, of course, but also a *cannabinoid celebration*. Or in soccer, when I see a player flush from scoring a goal, the moment with the big grin and look of success, I see someone high on their body and anandamide. When I see someone *"in the zone,"* athletic talk for intuitively hot playing, I see the focus of the runner's high and a body grooving. The zone is *cannabinoid dependent*: it surely is not, as the science on this is convincing, it surely is not *cannabinoid independent*.

In the *Runner's World* interview, President Bush credits some counseling from Reverend Billy Graham on quitting drinking. He said: *"It's well-documented that Billy Graham provided* **the spiritual contrast of the body temple** *which allowed me to convince myself to stop drinking."* (Bold added)

That is true, for President Bush and the rest of us, and without any guarantor of value - *my body is my temple*. There is a disconnect and bridge missing in our current thinking if we deny the role of cannabinoids in human health. It's like thinking our world is flat or the center of the universe when we know it is round and orbits the sun.

That ends this beginning.

Aphorisms on value

Book 1

1

At a loss. Wither the peace child and wither Christianity.

2

Puking. People will opt for regurgitation over rumination. Some would rather puke than think about it. It should be common knowledge that humans are capable of anything. This means we live possibilities. It sounds simple enough, but to take it in as a measure is often cumbersome. Individuals tend to think differently. This means they think in terms of knowledge and not possibilities. But knowledge is much less abundant in our day-to-day lives than possibility. When knowledge realizes that possibility is a recurring phenomenon (all phenomenon are recurring), then it demands less rumination.

3

Selling out. A sellout crowd is positive and always underrepresented – as more wanted in. A sellout individual, on the other hand, is usually negative. A sellout is someone who surrenders. With some Christians it is even a mark of faith – sold out to Jesus, and that kind of selling out. With oligarchy, we have sold out our seats. With large districts, we've made campaigns prohibitively expensive, which makes money a necessity, and, for all practical purpose, keeps the locals down.

4

God Bless America. A nation that prays for vengeance, which is referred to as justice and victory, and then gets vengeance, that nation will have a stronger belief in God. In the mind of the believer, victory after prayer validates prayer – thus reinforcing the idea of God.

5

Divided we fall. The slogan, *"United we stand, divided we fall,"* was a national motto. Now it's shorter and stronger. There is no room for division in the war on terror. *United we stand.*

6

Aborigine wars. The United States fought the aborigine wars by fomenting violence and terror. We utilized policies that pitted tribe against tribe, thereby weakening both, and relying on our ever-vast and ever-increasing resources, we possessed and have developed their homeland and now call it ours. This fact is rarely discussed, as we prefer pioneering stories such as Lincoln and his log splitting. Even more than our institution of slavery, it is what we like to misremember: our founding's *war of terror.*

The morality of the aborigine wars doesn't interest me much. The people and tribes are gone; instead we have farms, small towns, and cities like Philadelphia, Chicago, Denver, Los Angeles, and Seattle. Nature and culture proceeded hand in hand: it was in our nature and culture to take their homeland.

7

Horses. Horses drove the pre-industrial growth in the United States, and literally, they made the movement west possible. Even the first two railway companies, the Granite Railway Company of Quincy, Massachusetts (1826) and Baltimore's B & O (1830), utilized horses to pull cars on the tracks. The horse was to be less and less of an influence with the invention of the steam-powered engine.

8

Federalized mono-regency. If you look at international relations, we are witnessing world government in action. It is a federalized mono-regency much like the state governor system in the US. Mono-regent systems that open their borders to our culture and who recognize the borders of other mono-regencies are considered tributary allies. They can pay tribute in blood like the Northern Alliance did in Afghanistan, or like the French, in disgruntled support, who arrived in Mazar-Shariff three weeks after the fighting had ended.

9

Here's my love of America. We won't understand what we are doing if we don't understand what we are capable of doing. We are conquerors. We conquered this land we now call home. Not you and me, and not even our grandparents, but it was done in the name of our country and under our flag. Many have fallen defending our flag, and many have fallen fighting it.

Purdue University plays a smoothie-type song before home football games called, *"I am an American."* It talks of midwestern skies, bravery and pride, but not the conquered. As Americans, we are conquerors. The word has fallen out of use, as we prefer champion or venture capitalist, but conquering is what we do good: Iroquois, Winnebago, Illiniwek, Crow, Mandan, Blackfeet, Apache/Tinneh, Comanche, Shawnee, Ioway, Sauk,

Kaskaskia, Potawatomi, Kickapoo, Miami, Chippewa, Ottawa, Erie, Delaware, Kishwaukee, Lakota, Fox/Meskquakies, Sioux, . . . ><

10

I'm not a moralizer. We cannot change the past or even the present. Let's focus on the future, on the time we have before us. Time itself is immoral, and there is much we can learn from it – the seamlessness of it – and not.

11

Standard time. In 1883, the railroad companies in the United States got together and created Standard Time. In order to make the trains run on schedule, they needed a way to bridge towns like Davenport, Iowa to Columbus, Ohio via the railroad line. So, on 18 November 1883, the day referred to as *The Day of Two Noons*, railway clocks across the country were set to one hour apart in four time zones: Eastern, Central, Mountain and Pacific. Soon, state and local officials followed the new system; it wasn't until 35 years later, in 1918, that the federal government codified the change into law with the Standard Time Act.

12

Dissembling. When facing an absolutist, take an absolutist position. The absolutist cannot compromise – that's what makes him or her an absolutist. The absolutist will be left looking at two options: they will be viewed as intolerant (as they are) or they will compromise. In either case, something may have been learned. If you aren't an absolutist, compromise is just part of the day.

13

Too much. It really is too much. The God of monotheism will destroy other clans and tribes for worshipping idols – symbols really, and often made of stone – and what does the God of monotheism want in return for the promise? He asked for a symbol – a mark – from the boys and men. Evidence for this, we are told, is found in Genesis 17:10-14. There is also mention of mass adult circumcision in Genesis 34. Too much.

14

Unfaith. Faithless has gotten a bad name over the years. It should mean, at a basic level, without faith. At one time faith simply meant "to trust." That was before science. Christian faith has taken this to another level, mainly because of science. One has faith in Jesus as the messiah, the other has experiential learning. Put simply, one kind of faith says he is risen – the other kind of faith says show me the evidence.

Synonyms for *faithless* paint a dreary matrix – making the faithless appear untrustworthy. Some common equivalents to faithless are unfaithful, false, disloyal, traitorous, inconstant, fickle and undependable.

The faithless, those who do not adhere firmly and devotedly, as to a person, cause, or idea – the faithless have unfaith. They disbelieve. What definition is the positive of unfaith? – Perhaps to adhere to the firm and unfounded, to the devoted and undevoted, as to a person, cause or idea. *Unfaith* is a withholding of the urge to trust, and it is as human as faith.

15

Terrorism. One of the blames for our current war on terror (remember, the British burned Washington D.C. and the "Indians" burned our frontier and killed our settlers, and Sherman burned Georgia, and so on) is our lack of human intelligence. We don't have anyone on the inside, and they obviously do. We have been told that by getting inside – better intelligence from spying – that we will better understand them. Understanding them is important: understanding ourselves is also. Perhaps "getting inside" is an old war strategy, and our president says the war on terror is the first war of the 21st century. Perhaps we should think differently. Here's one – with approximately zero Arab-Americans in our House, and estimates ranging from two to six million in the country, what if we had *Constitutional Representation*? – Then some of "them" would be in the House and we would gain intelligence. We may even find that they are less "them" and more "us." Perhaps, in lacking the human intelligence a constitutionally represented House would provide, we also lack what's needed to make peace.

16

Rome. The Rome of Paul's time and America have much in common. World leaders in economics, law, and military might, one could say we live in Rome's shadow. I would be anti-Christian if it mattered, but it doesn't. If war was the answer, why didn't Jesus lead his disciples into battle? The Zealots did, not Jesus. Muhammad did, not Jesus.

I am reminded of something Baudrillard wrote in a small book called *Forget Foucault*: "*The imminence of the death of all the great referents (religious, sexual, political, etc.) is expressed by exacerbating the forms of violence and representation that characterized them. There is no doubt that fascism, for example, is the first obscene and pornographic form of a desperate 'revival' of political power.*"

17

Addiction. Death is less interesting once you've lived. It takes a lot of time and energy to think about one's death. I've done plenty of it; probably more than needed, and in the end, what can you say? – One lives, one dies.

Living has become endless. The possible burdens me and not the impossible – the after world of whatever. Burdens is perhaps too strong, but not also somewhat true. The burden comes in the form of paranoia. Like the Kinks said, it can destroy you.

Paranoia is an ugly piss-ant of a beast. The bite of a termite comes to mind as it gnaws on something good. Paranoia is an unlit filled room. It is consciously unlit, consciously without light for the eyes. In the unlit filled room, there is a sucking sound coming from different directions. This sucking sound sucks. When you think in the possible, with the sucking sound in the background whirling away, you have to make peace with paranoia. You see, paranoia is the shadow of the possible. It, paranoia, is a paradox: it lacks light and needs it to exist. Like a shadow, if paranoia is given too much light – or none at all – it disappears. So there are two ways to effectively deal with paranoia –

bring it into the light or none at all. The same technique and strategy can work on habits that lead to dependence and problems. I recently heard someone say, "*dependence plus problem equals addiction,*" and that makes sense to me.

18

Apache. Maybe the United States will never be able to see the aborigine for what they were: people who lost their world to ours. We don't have to moralize it and call ourselves great or evil. It is what we are, and we'd be wise to know ourselves. In *The American Indian Wars, 1860-1890,* a cavalry officer fighting the "Apache" had this to say: "*With a stupidity strictly consistent with the whole history of our contact with the aborigines, the people of the United States have maintained a bitter and unrelenting warfare against a people whose name was unknown to them. The Apache is not the Apache: the name 'Apache' does not occur in the language of the 'Tinneh', by which name . . . our Indian prefers to designate himself 'The Man'.*"

The word "Apache" is Zuni for enemy.

19

Sex. Since the sins of the father and mother are passed onto the new born, thus the need for the baptism ritual, there is no innocence in Christianity. This appears counter-intuitive, but is not: Christians defend the idea of innocence, yet Christian faith precludes and negates innocence since all are sinners (even the fetus in the womb). That's why they baptize them so young and why Christians generally oppose abortion.

There is something perverse about being the sacrificial Son of God the Father. I mean, didn't Jesus have to wonder about a God-the-Father-created system that calls upon the sacrifice of a son? I would have been like, "*Dad, what's up with that?*"

Circumcision – now, ouch, there's a touchy subject. The Old Testament says Abraham circumcised himself when he was 99. He did this as his part of the covenant with God. God demanded it - the mark of God on the penis – to fulfill the covenant. Genesis 17:10-14 says to do this on the 8th day after birth. This may be heresy, I know, but didn't God the Father put the foreskin there just eight days or nine months before? After an initial welcome and hello, *He* wants it back? – Hmm.

Let's say Jesus is twelve and he sees a pregnant woman. Does he understand he was created by a visit from the Holy Ghost and not made from Mary and Joseph? Is the difference apparent to him? Did the kids tease him and call him the "Holy Ghost Child"? Did he get hangnails? If he did, did they heal quickly? When did he realize he had intuitions and talents that the other humans didn't? In other words, did he ever lose at such childhood games as hide-and-go-seek?

You see, that is one of the problems and strengths of Christianity: the focus on the young. Circumcision is recommended for the boys and baptism for all babies. By the 8th grade there has been Sunday school, Christmas, Easter, traditions, births, marriages and death, all with a Christian theme. Then there is confirmation into the congregation. By the age of fourteen, you are a member of the flock.

Of course, other than the circumcision, all of these experiences are not negative in the whole. That means they serve other purposes as well. For many Americans these have been life-forming experiences. I for one went through them all. The problem for Christianity is that it is in direct competition with modernism. Jesus as a human doesn't have an issue with modernism; Jesus as the messiah, well, then he does.

Jesus Christ has beaten me down for years, but no more: his ideal sacrifice no longer sways me. For me, it appeared in repression, anger and lust – in trying to be Christ-like. Then there is failing and sin. More attempts to live by the book, but the failing repeats and so does the efforts to live by the book. Each failing ingrains Christ into your consciousness. You become hailed, that is, called by Jesus. Soon, I was just waiting to die.

20

More so. Humans love dialectics; some even think we wouldn't know what to do without them.

Christianity is a lifestyle. So is following the Qur'an. So is exercising your cannabinoid system. When it comes to those who use plant cannabinoids, we enact, tolerate, and justify laws targeting a minority population – cannabis consumers. Even more so, we enact, tolerate, and justify laws targeting a minority within cannabis consumers – young black men. This desire by the government to punish cannabis users is rooted in the idea that a state has the right and moral obligation to protect the public; make cannabis evil, morally, and then you can keep punishing the users. Same model will work for Muslims.

Cannabis has uses, which is a fact that is often lost in moral debates. Often, the absolutist who believes in the Fall of humans cannot allow the right to get high, or the right to ease pain, or the right to walk upright for five minutes a day. Yeah, the absolutist cannot have that. They want you "low," in pain, and slouched. As moralizers they are simply more pessimistic than I am. Since the Fall, humans await the day of Judgement. My *tragic passionism* makes me look like the eternal optimist. Perhaps, to the absolutist, I am the *tragic passionist,* since I remain bridged to this world and not the next.

21

Lifestyle. In Lake County, Illinois, there lives a blind woman who suffers from multiple sclerosis, corneal lattice dystrophy, and glaucoma. At her trial for growing marijuana, the prosecutor representing the people of Illinois, told the judge about posters celebrating cannabis culture; he mentioned a Bob Marley poster with the quote, *"Emancipate yourself from mental slavery, none but ourselves can free our minds,"* and pictures of the woman's teenage daughter and son in front of the plants. The prosecutor said this pattern of behavior pointed to more than medicinal use and toward *"a lifestyle."*

The same ideology that raided this woman, prohibition, also killed a man in a Lake County McDonald's parking lot. He died over a $50 cocaine deal gone wrong. He was killed by an undercover police officer after the coke user thought the officer was going to rob him – or something – he panicked and was killed by gunfire. Our laws create violent confrontations rather than lessening them. We tax and regulate pharmaceuticals: no reason to treat other medicines differently.

And yes, it is about *lifestyle* – some of us want a *life less-styled by violence*.

22

Power is something exchanged. In *Forget Foucault*, Baudrillard writes of power as something that is exchanged. In our small House of Representatives, this means power has been consolidated in the oligarchy and exchanged for incumbent power. For a constitutional House of Representatives, a large House, power would be consolidated in many Representatives and exchanged for local, that is dispersed, power. The idea was to disperse factions and power to a central/federal government to calm the people: *the power principle in the Constitution is gathering factions best festering factions.*

Baudrillard also writes: *"challenge is the opposite of dialogue: it creates a nondialectic, ineluctable space. It is neither means nor end: it opposes its own space to political space."*

23

Cannabinoids and Cholesterol. The human body makes both cannabinoids and cholesterol. Foods containing cholesterol are not felonious, yet we know for a fact that cholesterol, in the wrong amounts, can kill you. This makes it senseless to prohibit foods containing cannabinoids, which are nontoxic and helpful for lots of things. *Be human.*

24

Future of science/nonscience. In an aphorism called the "Future of science," Nietzsche said the next culture, often called the *"higher culture,"* will need a double brain – two sides – one for science and one for nonscience. The two sides will have to work together: *"one to experience science, and one to experience nonscience."*

According to Nietzsche these two sides of a brain will have to lie together: *"Lying next to one another, without confusion, separable, self-contained"* – he suggests – *"our health demands this."* It is this demand on health, on the body, that is interesting. The demand is upon us, as the next culture will make humans experience science and nonscience. It is this demand on the body, on health, that is present. Here's what Nietzsche said about this demand:

> *If this demand made by higher culture is not satisfied, we can almost certainly predict the further course of human development: interest in truth will cease, the less it gives pleasure; illusion, error, and fantasies, because they are linked with pleasure, will reconquer their former territory step by step; the ruin of the sciences and relapse into barbarism follow next. Mankind will have to begin to weave its cloth from the beginning again, after having, like Penelope, destroyed it in the night. But who will guarantee that we will keep finding the strength to do so?*

Pleasure is found in science, in searching for truth. It is also found in illusion, error, and fantasies. Pleasure makes no distinction between the two. If the truth is no longer fun, if it no longer brings pleasure, humans will just as likely turn to something else – to another pleasure.

25

Religion and philosophy. The needs of religion and philosophy – the needs of Abraham and Socrates – are the same. As needs, they can be weeded out. This process can be disturbing and long, or as short as a trip if you have the right provisions. The needs can be satisfied, eliminated, and/or made scientific: to satisfy, feed them; to eliminate, fast; to make scientific, stop complaining and glorifying the world (it is what it is and so are we).

26

Pleasure. What is it you do for fun? It is a common experience, pleasure, but one that comes in an infinite multitude of forms. The word "forms" doesn't carry the punch we want, does it? But capturing pleasure itself, in a word or otherwise, is often difficult. How about: *explosive in an orgasmic way.*

27

Intentions. God never had intentions prior to monotheism.

28

Sodomy laws. There's an old saying about getting out of people's lives: it's *"Get out of people's lives!"* We've grown intrusive when we criminalize the simple possession of a plant. Worse than sodomy laws, where the police have to catch you in the act, with cannabis, it's all about possession.

29

Hope is disabling. I haven't used the concept hope much. It is a human emotion experienced by millions. Hope is disabling: it has the power to make still. When used on fear, it can disable it. That is how it is used to perfection.

30

Racism. It's like saying racism is about race instead of power. It isn't about race: it's about ignorance, inertia and resistance to change. Racism is a "custom" – a habit we've grown into and one we'll outgrow.

31

Writer/Worder. Writing is a conversation with time. It is putting words on paper the way a painter covers canvas. Instead of "writer," it would also be accurate to say "worder."

32

The Rush Syndrome. I like to think of all the things individuals do when they are legally cannabinoid impaired. You see, in this state, Illinois, you are legally "impaired" if you have any of a particular cannabinoid in your body. When they say, "driving under the influence of cannabis," they really mean, "driving under the past use of cannabis," as that is all their test can show (past use). They measure for the cannabinoid metabolite

Carboxy-THC, a metabolite produced by the body. Science doesn't have a good theory why the body stores the metabolite for up to a month in fat. Perhaps it plays a role in health; the body usually stores things in fat that will be used later (stored energy). Perhaps this cannabinoid metabolite will play a bigger role in understanding the human cannabinoid system and health than it has in the measurement of past use as impairment.

Cannabis laws discriminate along the lines of consumption. If you consume in the proper endocannabinoid way, you are praised. Consume in the exogenous plant way and be arrested. It should be noted, but very expensive, it is legal to consume exocannabinoids made by pharmaceutical companies and obtained by prescriptions – such as *Dronabinol* (Marinol®, synthetic THC: delta-9-tetrahydrocannabinol) and *Nabilone* (Cesament®, synthetic THC analogue). It might be the powers that make these decisions don't trust the people with a plant – or it could be *The Rush Syndrome*, named after Rush Limbaugh, for perfect rational public life, drug using private life, and all is good except the illegality.

33

The myth of super weed. Sure, it's out there, this super weed with its outlandishly high THC content. The cannabis plant is as varied as any other. Look at all the kinds of corn, thistles, or tomatoes – the plant world, like our own, varies.

Super weed is expensive and rare. Think of the best and sweetest ear of corn or the largest and juiciest tomato: they exist but are uncommon. Cannabis works the same way. Super cannabis is rare, for sure, but it is even harder to abuse, if that is the concern. The body can only take in so much cannabis; when the receptors are full, the body talks through your consciousness to say "I'm good" or "No thanks" and you pass. Of course, some consume too much: *that happens with or without super weed.* Alcohol, if we look around us, is more of a danger and does far more harm; it sets its users up for failure. At my age, I'm seeing the beginning of a new generation of alcohol drinking. On it goes.

There are many types of alcohol drunks. There's the wine drunk, gin drunk, whiskey drunk, beer drunk, the popular beer and whiskey drunk, and on and on for a very long list of alcohol drunks. We can draw a parallel to cannabis here, as the genetics of the plant determine the kind of cannabis you will have; different cannabis will have different cannabinoids. Also, the human cannabinoid system varies, as each human is unique; for example, the same cannabis will have different effects depending on the consumer, and the same is true of alcohol. This means we are not all wired the same, that not all cannabinoid systems are created equal. One puff on a pipe or one gram of a brownie is good for some; a joint or four grams of a brownie is good for others. Why super weed is a myth is because it posits fear as its credentials when knowledge and understanding are also available. Stronger cannabis like stronger alcohol, can be understood for what it is – a consumable. Watching what we consume is just part of being human, so consume well.

34

No taxation without representation. During the American Revolution, the concept *No taxation without representation* rallied and unified *We the People.*

35

Genesis 1:29. In the beginning of the Old Testament, God told the early writers to include this line, found in Genesis 1:29, "*And God said, Behold, I have given you every herb bearing seed, which is upon the face of all the earth, and every tree, in which is the fruit of a tree yielding seed; to you it shall be for meat.*"

Cannabis sativa is a seed bearing plant that you can eat.

36

The means – human, all too human. Do not think this with ease: human, all too human is a means to understanding humans (yourself included) through psychological observations. It involves thinking and you have to know your body. There is no secret, there is no magic, not necessarily so, but it might often feel like there is; that's just the future beckoning you – and that's a feeling and a means.

37

Genius. Nietzsche put it this way in 1878, not about America or our ways, but about getting anything done: "*The genius, too, does nothing other than first learn to place stones, then to build, always seeking material, always forming and reforming.*"

38

Mussolini. Speaking to the US Senate in 1929 while debating the *Decennial Census and Apportionment of Representatives Act,* the one about having only *435* Representatives and also referred to as the *Permanent Apportionment Act,* a Senator Black brought up the notion of liberty. I mention this as a reminder that people often have different preferences and goals. Senator Black's words about free people:

> *I realize, as do many others, that there is a great deal of sentiment all over this Nation in favor of Mussolini running Italy, because, they say, he establishes order and security. There are people who bow down at the shrine of order and security and who forget that liberty is and has been all down the ages more valuable than are order and security.*

Just a reminder: keep the past as well as the present and future in mind.

39

Norte Chico. Recent archaeological findings tell us of another story of adaptation and a previously unknown civilization in South America, called *Norte Chico.* One look at the dates of this civilization and the more and more we begin to notice this world, the so-called New World, isn't so new after all. Yes, this world here, the one in the Americas, is getting older. The Norte Chico civilization began around 3,000 BC – making it older than most civilizations found in the lands called holy. Recently, on the coast of Peru, scientists have found evidence that the Norte Chico world lasted 1,200 years, as they successfully moved from a hunter and gathering group to one that created more than 20 urban areas – making their longevity as a civilization more than the Maya, Aztec and Inca combined.

40

"You can't run away from yourself" (Bob Marley). Have you ever tried running away from yourself? Hard to do really, and in the end you really don't get very far. You can't really do the other either, the opposite – you can't really run toward or to yourself. You can be yourself – there, that's it.

Aphorisms on value

Book 2

41

What a lark. A new Illinois state law: the soda (pop) machines (Pepsi, Coke) must be inoperable during lunch period; by law, they must be turned off. Instead of teaching our students good habits – no excessive soda drinking – we make it illegal to purchase.

42

Fear. Drug warriors motivate by fear. Drug warriors and drug reformers share the fact that we don't want kids doing drugs. What we differ on is approach: warriors will deny federal student loans to drug offenders as a form of punishment; reformers prefer education about drugs, or knowledge instead of punishment (fear).

43

Science of drugs. All these drugs, but so little science: cannabis, Ritalin, caffeine, alcohol, sugar and all the others, they're a part of our future. In fact, drugs are our future, for better and worse, so we might as well be knowledgeable. Knowledge over myth, as science beats fear.

44

Guilt. We didn't do enough to stop the Holocaust, but we feel less guilt when it comes to the aborigine and Manifest Destiny, where we did a lot more we should feel guilty about. A sign of America's *will* to not know.

45

Manifest Destiny. The idea that the United States was going somewhere was bound up in the idea of Manifest Destiny. Beginning with the thirteen colonies/states, we added three more states by the end of the 18th century. In the 19th century we added 29 states – Utah being the last at forty-five. In the 20th century, things began to slow down with five states added – the last was Hawaii on 21 August 1959. Maybe this is one of the problems, one of those lost goals. Maybe we should open the process up again and return to the vim and vigor of the theory of Manifest Destiny. Instead of a free Iraq, perhaps we should invite them to join as the 51st state and the first of the 21st century (if Puerto Rico doesn't want it) and then they would be a part of us. That would make Iraq a state of the United States. Imagine – and then recall that no one really thought thirteen colonies would so soon become a world power.

46

Three fifths of all other Persons. The US Constitution, its writers and those who voted to support it, valued the slave, another human, as sixty percent of a white person. I wondered as a kid what forty percent did slaves lack? Did they think slaves lacked *a little here* and *a little there* and it added up to a forty percent reduction? Did slaves just lack some qualities in general, such as a sense of moral right and wrong? I can imagine the debate by the best and the brightest (which they were): "Dear sirs: I make a motion that the slaves should be counted as two thirds of a person and not three fifths. Slaves . . ." See the codification of value? Do we think it out of our possibility to create value? That is what the founders did and it is what we all do – and we even make colossal errors in judgement. Their judgement and compromise codified intolerance and prejudice. Today we find the conclusion *three fifths of all other Persons* to be morally bankrupt; by the standards of 1787, it was a compromise.

47

Nuclear World 2004.
1) US, Britain and Israel: three nuclear nations running over nonnuclear nations and peoples – Afghanistan, Iraq and the Palestinians.
2) Iran: going nuclear thanks to our allies.
3) India and Pakistan: gone nuclear.
4) North Korea: gone nuclear and daring us to stop them from more.
5) History: the US is the only nation to use nuclear weapons in war.

48

Change. If you've ever tried to change someone's opinion about anything, perhaps you'll find this wisdom from Tolstoy to be helpful:

> *I know that most men, including those at ease with problems of the greatest complexity, can seldom accept even the simplest and most obvious truth if it be such as would oblige them to admit the falsity of conclusions which they have delighted in explaining to colleagues, which they have proudly taught to others, and which they have woven, thread by thread, into the fabric of their lives.*

49

Tyranny. It has been said no majority should be able to persecute a minority. That is an example of an ideal, and as a model, they can be useful. As a model, mind you, as a model: reality is another thing.

50

Straight to love. Going through monotheism to get to love wastes energy and time. Go straight to love – it's efficient.

51

To be human. Evolution is a dead end for all other living things, so why would humans be the exception? We're not. The idea of progress dead ends just like all other ideas do. It too will one day be extinct. There is no point to life, and yet there is an end. My life always means our life, as there is no my without our.

52

Iowa. We moved what remained of Black Hawk's tribe to the Iowa Territory, but they didn't fair well there either: the last tribes were moved out of Iowa in 1851. Since the first white settler in Iowa, Julien Dubuque, didn't arrive until 1788, well, that means the aborigine were moved out of Iowa in a quick 63 years and the US "acquired" more than 56,000 square miles of land and called it *Iowa* – which is what the aborigine *Ioway* called the *Iowa River*.

Our way, the American way, killed the aborigine. We won, they lost. No moral victory. The terror imposed on the aborigine broke many of the Ten Commandments. For sure we broke *thou shalt not kill* and *thou shalt not covet*.

53

Fascism. My dad on food – something he says he struggles with – he says: "It's good when you're up and it's good when you're down."

Fascism comes from fear – no fear, no fascism. We court disaster in a major defeat – an event that would foster fascism. I'm not fear mongering – fear of fascism – I just wanted to make sure we understand it can grow anywhere – it is a human emotion, and the myths of pastoral America must be seen in the light of the aborigine, slavery, lynchings, vigilantism, and so on – the good and the bad. It is mythical to think fascism cannot grow here or anywhere. There is nothing in any nation's DNA to make it immune to the flaring up of fear when a people feel threatened.

54

Chemistry. If you posit a God, a creator, or an intelligent design model, whatever you think of humans and how we got here, whatever it Is, it's the best chemist in the history of the universe.

55

Verse. There is a connection, verbally, about our word "universe" and the Delphic Oracle. The first speakers there spoke in verse – they chanted in verse. That's how we are told things began there.

56

Death. I have long understood that funerals are for the living: the dead don't care. The living mourn and move on the best they can. That is why funerals have a bright future; in times of distress and sadness, they fill a void.

57

Bible and Constitution. Maybe my brain is tweaked from thinking about this, but why have a Bible and Constitution you don't use in times of distress? That is exactly when they should be used.

"The Middle East" means something in the context of *east* and *west*, the binary twins of *north* and *south*, but without a determination like the equator that neatly slices the two. The equator acts as a moderator between *north* and *south*; *east* and *west* have only the dateline, a human invention lacking the power of magnetic pull. It zigs and zags its way across the Pacific Ocean without completing the circle. Time lacks magnetism: geographically, it has no center.

58

Wasted time. There is no wasted time. To say it is wasted is to moralize it, which is always after the time has expired.

Why did people believe the world was flat when the sun and moon were round? Or did they think it was flat and round? As Ezra Pound said, commentators create their own Eden.

We are mistaken in the belief that September 11th is like December 7th. The 7th was an attack by military people on military people. The 11th was an attack by civilians on civilians. The hijackers were civilians trained to be militant. They have more in common with, and we honestly learn more about their frame of mind, to see them as kamikaze pilots. Like the guy arrested in Minnesota, the kamikazes didn't care about landing the plane.

The individuals killed in the attacks of September 11th died real and symbolic deaths. I want to be clear here: I mean everyone, hijackers included. We may not understand, and too often we even mock their use of *jihad*, but it is a real and symbolically important act. Recall the towers came down, the Pentagon was pierced, and the White House and Capitol were under threat.

The 11th should be compared, as much as these comparisons function to frame our awareness, around the events of and after the assassination of the Archduke Ferdinand. A Bosnian revolutionary assassinated the heir to the Austrian and Hungarian thrones and his wife Sophie. Today we would call him a terrorist. The events of 28 June 1914 would transform world politics. As they say, the world was never the same.

The Archduke's assassination set in motion the events and deaths of World War I. The crater in New York is the latest ground zero to drive nations. The loss of life was terrible, but it is the loss of symbolic security (the real and imagined) that makes many tremble.

The loss of symbolic security numbs; it's in numbness we kill. The richest nation in the world bombing one of the poorest isn't a great victory ... it's a defeat.

We make a blunder if we let the enemy choose the grounds for war. Picking when to fight is more important than how. Our strength is time and technology, not the shedding of volunteer blood. There is no necessity for national bloodlust; it is certainly a possibility and throughout our history there's been a tendency (willingness) to shed blood (ours and others) for national survival and growth. Yet strength exhibits patience, as it has time on its side (think of Hud); time spent waiting is often better than hasty bomb dropping.

59

A common phrase. "Love the sinner, hate the sin," is a common phrase in America among Christians: the sin usually refers to homosexuality. This, of course, has always been a bit of a misnomer, but at least it offered some love. I suppose I dream of an America where that is the least amount of joy we can show to those who are "different." Difference doesn't have to involve sin. For example, those suffering and who want to try cannabis to ease their symptoms – difference doesn't necessitate sin. In fact, it is sinful to cause undo pain to another human being, isn't it?

60

Nothing in everything. In being everything, God is also nothing – as the category "everything" has to include every-thing, and nothing is a thing. For the Is, this doesn't create a problem, as everything and nothing are in the same category – a thing, possible – just like 1 and –1.

61

Terrain. The Confederate General Robert E. Lee did not lose many battles. He didn't lose because he was brilliant at choosing on what grounds the battle would be waged, and thus controlled to the best that one can how the battle would be fought. But when fighting in enemy territory, near the towns of Sharpsburg in Maryland and Gettysburg in Pennsylvania, for example, he lost his edge. On his first venture, near Sharpsburg, he was only saved from defeat by a cornfield, a sunken road, and a bridge over Antietam stream that was used to hold off the Union army. Confederate General A.P. Hill's soldiers arrived as the sun was setting and saved Lee's army from destruction.

62

The history of stone worshipping. If we were to write a history of stone worshipping, it would be a very long history.

63

Surrender. I surrender, what are your terms? This nation needs a peace conference on cannabis – drug war peace would be the theme.

64

This isn't Phish tour! On "Phish tour" means you follow the band awhile, city to city, venue to venue, and take in the scene – hang with other freaks, so to speak, and experience that. Some people stay on tour a week, some a summer, some a year, and even a few lifers. On Phish tour, things can take a carefree attitude. When you get home from such a trip, it can take a while to adapt back to things. At home, you can put the experiences into your own frame – into your Is, so to speak. It's not like your experience will be my experience. In a group of particulars that may be the case – similar stories told differently – but in the whole, there's no resolution, nothing to resolve.

Some people like to stay on tour – that means that is how they live and organize their Is. That is also part of our Is, just a different way of saying how things are. Nietzsche said that with the loss of God and a move toward constitutionalism, he said constitutional governments were signs of compromise and that they transformed as well. He said that without God as a guarantor of value: *"justice must become greater in everyone, and the violent instinct weaker."*

65

Keanna Mattox. It's hard to lose someone. Keanna was a student of mine at Holy Trinity High School in Chicago. She was killed by gunfire; the headline in the Metro section of the Chicago Tribune said, "Party shooting kills girl, 15." She was pronounced dead at 6:35 a.m. in Stroger Hospital as reported by a Cook County medical examiner.

Keanna, "Keke" to her friends, was at the proverbial wrong place at the wrong time. Her wrong place was outside a party where a gun was present, and her wrong time was 12:52 a.m., 21 August 2004. This was during the end of her summer vacation, that time between her ninth and tenth grades. She was shot in the abdomen and lived less than six hours. The paper reported things I already knew. Her friends told the reporter that she had a great sense of humor and style and she always made a bad situation better. She was like that.

Justice must become greater in everyone, and the violent instinct weaker.

66

Sedulous. Think of yourself as diligent and painstaking. Make change.

67

Marking beginnings. Let's say it all began on 11 September 2001. Look at a list of nations involved in recent war spots and tell me if you see a world war beginning: the United States, Afghanistan, United Kingdom, Israel, Italy, Spain, Poland, Iraq, Russia, Bulgaria, Saudi Arabia, Yemen, Germany, Chechnya, Lebanon, Syria, Indonesia, Palestine, Kuwait, Ukraine, Japan, India, Jordan . . .

68

Faith? Those who could not trust invented faith. Faith is common among the unconvinced – those who lack conviction in a particular idea or group of ideas.

69

Killings, guns, and bombs. Peace, like war, is a human condition. There is nothing more magical about it than war. For either condition to be present they must be nurtured, that is brought along and to life. The United States has not been good at nurturing peace.

The last declared wars were on 8 December 1941, the day after Pearl Harbor, and on 11 December 1941, after Germany and Italy declared war on the US and we reciprocated. So that makes 11 December 1941, the last time our Constitution was used to declare war. Sixty years, and yet we've fought around the world. No war declared on Korea or Vietnam. No war declared on Cambodia or Laos. No war in Desert Shield and Desert Storm. No war in Serbia or Kosovo. No war on terror has been declared, at least not constitutionally. President Roosevelt went to Congress and asked them to declare war on Imperial Japan, as they referred to it back then. After Germany and Italy said war to us, he asked again for the declarations. Both times he got them, almost unanimously.

On 25 September 2001, as the war preparations for Afghanistan continued, the operation was renamed. Several leading Islamic scholars pointed out that Bush's first choice, "Operation Infinite Justice," was overdone. They said *infinite justice* was in God's realm. Bush fixed it by renaming it, "Operation Enduring Freedom."

The heady term "infinite justice" deserves some discussion. His father, President George H. Bush, was content with names like, "Operation Desert Shield" and "Operation Desert Storm." In trying to imagine infinite justice, where does one start? One would have to consider the philosophical and legal traditions concerning the concepts of *infinite* and *justice*, along with such ideas as *finite* and *unjust*, and include a working knowledge of the Old and New Testaments and the Qur'an. The meanings in combination are endless. Maybe that was the intention – long-term war, a so-called endless war; perhaps, because what cannot be defined or sustained without abstraction – as in the concept *infinite justice*, which logically negates itself – he was thinking of operationalizing. Maybe the change was a blessing.

70

Complete determinatus. Kant wrote pithy aphorisms. One of my favorites is #100 in *Critique of Pure Reason – Analytic and synthetic definition.* The one before it, simply *Definition*, tells us what he expected from a definition. This is no small means; Kant was big on definitions, defined as, "a sufficiently distinct and precise concept." In Latin, which he provided, it reads: "*conceptus rei adaequatos in minimis terminis, complete determinatus.*" This is then rendered in a footnote: "a concept adequate to the thing, in minimal terms, completely determined." Kant believed the definition to be "a logically perfect concept." Clear, yes?

In the 100th aphorism, in a section on "Furthering Logical Perfection of Cognition Thought Definition, Exposition, and Description of Concepts," he writes two sentences about analytic and synthetic definition. Don't mind all the Kantian verbiage here (Nietzsche called him the great delayer); do notice my italics on the four "be" verbs he used: "All definitions *are* either analytic or synthetic. The former *are* definitions of a concept that *is given*, the latter of one that *is made*."

All this being – *are, are, is, is* – and the transitive verbs of doing – *given and made* – all this being isn't done in a vacuum. Plus: how often are four acts of being ever completely determined? There is a body doing the doing, and it is rarely, if ever, that well known. That is what the Kantian system cannot account for – *the incompletely determined*. Humans are determined, yes, but rarely, if ever, completely.

71

Misrepresentative. It's just not true to think we live by a Constitution that we don't live by. If under the threat of war our Constitution is weak, who really believes it will work well in times of peace? So let's clarify: the US House International Relations Committee believes that giving President Bush, or any president, the authority needed to use force: *"is the best way to avoid its use."* It would seem on the surface somewhat absurd to think that giving someone the ability to use force would be the best way to avoid its use. Doesn't the counter to this logic make more sense – that not giving the president the authority he needs to use force is the best way to avoid its use? Apparently I'm missing something – like the logic of this argument. I find it hard to believe that giving the president the "keys to the car," so to speak, is the best way to keep it from being used. The few suddenly become the fewest (one). That's not representative of *We the People*: it is misrepresentative, isn't it? The incumbents have always been playing with this number – for example, look at these two decades: the 1830 US population was 12 million and we had 240 Representatives; the 1860 population was 30 million and we had 241. That's 18 million more people counted and one Representative added. *(Note: the US Civil War began the following year, in 1861.)*

72

Plan your past. Folks talk about their past and they plan their future – what if they planned their past and talked about their future?

73

Some will say it's inconvenient. Inconvenience is not a reason to abrogate a constitution. Who said it wouldn't be inconvenient? The writers knew it would be: that's why on 8 August 1787, they inserted the words *"shall not exceed"* before *"one Representative for every forty Thousand."* They knew we would be dealing with factionalism: one wonders if the president, as executive and commander-in-chief, could unilaterally declare war if the House had 10,000 members. He (or she) could go on the latest hot medium – radio for Roosevelt - and address the nation and ask Congress to declare war; one can't do it unilaterally, at least not constitutionally. Think of that: we haven't declared war since Roosevelt. If a president can declare war, as this one has, then we no longer live under a constitutional government. If that is the truth, that the war-making power has shifted to the fewest (the president), well, that's *an unconstitutional "rule of law."* Hmm . . .

74

Ratification and statehood. The year 1889 was a good year for ratification of the Constitution in order to join the United States, as four new states entered the Union: North Dakota and South Dakota, which share the titles of 39th and 40th, Montana the 41st and Washington 42nd. The next year wasn't so bad either: in 1890 we added two more –

Idaho and Wyoming. It was also in 1890 that the Census Bureau declared the frontier to be closed.

75

The Leave Us (the fuck) Alone Party. If our House was made constitutional, then we would see the growth of alternative views. We might even see new parties form such as *LUAP* – *The Leave Us (the fuck) Alone Party.* I'd consider voting for candidates from LUAP.

76

Category slips. This is a human way of thinking, although I don't know how common. A person will not want to think of himself or herself as a particular thing, so one will mis-name what it is they are talking about. *It's a category slip.* Our Constitution fits here: we say one thing and do another.

What began in rebellion still rebels. The aborigine, French, Spanish, and British were our rivals, then Mexico, and along the way we kept displacing more and more aborigine with terror. We even had time to fight North and South in a civil war, a *white* war you could say. The last aborigine battle was at a place called Wounded Knee, South Dakota, in 1890.

With America's interior stabilized after 114 years of battle from without and within, we turned to the "external" stage with the Spanish-American War (1898). As we have seen, this is just an extension of war in general; it's *war* as policy, and it doesn't seem to end. The now external world of nation states is only possible after the internal world of tribes was secured.

77

Incomparable. If there is no guarantor of value, or the opposite, if there is a guarantor of value, or if it is some combination – one of contesting guarantors of value – the relationship between people and government will continue to evolve. Look at how it is different if power in government comes from a guarantor of value like God or a guarantor of value like individual citizens. In some ways they are incomparable: the former focuses on answering the question of the value of the whole, the latter looks at the accumulated particular – the known. As America shifts to a less providential government and to one where we see ourselves in it, we will notice more frequently that the secret at one time was that God guaranteed power; now power resides in us (Psalm 82 if needed), and the secret's been told many times. That's what kills a secret, not the secret, but in not keeping it. That's not a moral call, but as this develops, as more and more relationships come to be known as compromises – it's all compromises – then the concern over a guarantor of value dissipates and meaning is found not in it, in things, but in what we do with things. That's what Is.

78

Metaphysical Foundations of Natural Science. Many at the time thought that one of the key parts of Kant's *Critique of Pure Reason* – the part about "transcendental deduction of categories" – many thought it incomprehensible. That was 1781, and many still do. I do. But I do like how he, Kant, described the incomprehension in 1786, in his preface to the

Metaphysical Foundations of Natural Science, when he wrote: *"that part of the Critique which should have been the clearest was the most obscure, or even revolved in a circle."* Kant's problem revolved in a circle because he demanded pure reason to be circle free; but there is no reason, pure or otherwise, for a circle.

79

Monothinking. If you think there is a one, you are thinking in a mono way. That is human and can be observed using our senses. Thinking that there is a one is not of itself good or bad, as always, it is in the impact, in what we do with it. One God, one messiah, one Constitution, one body – none in their essence is good or bad – it depends on what we do with the thinking that matters.

80

Crows. Apollo, the Greek god of prophecy and keeper of the Delphic Oracle (when he wasn't sharing it with Dionysus), had a favorite group of birds. The story of the crow is one of change, for before one crow brought bad news to Apollo, all crows were white. (One wonders why the god of prophecy would need to be told anything?) The crow tells Apollo the truth – his lover, Coronis, a human, had slept with another human. For that, out of anger, Apollo not only turned this one crow black, but all crows.

The crow also played a mythical role in America's aboriginal customs – even the role of a deity, a god itself. The Shawnee have a story called *Why Crow is Black*, and it talks of how the original crow was white and that it came to be black by . . .

Ah yes, once again . . . the telling of familiar yet different stories.